THERESA V. WILSON

THE WRITER'S GUIDE
TO ACHIEVING SUCCESS:
A Workbook For Implementing The Plan

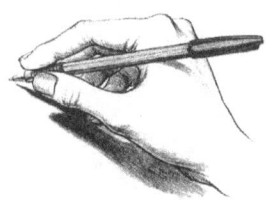

Writers in the Marketplace Press™
A subsidiary of VMAssociates, Inc.

2ND EDITION

Writers in the Marketplace™ Press
Subsidiary of VMAssociates, Inc.

Copyright ©2017 by Theresa V. Wilson, M.Ed., CPBA
ISBN# 978-0-692-98377-5

ALL RIGHTS RESERVED

Reproduction or translation of any part of this work beyond that permitted by Section 107 or 108 of the 1976 United States Copyright Act without the written permission of the copyright owner is unlawful.

Printed in the United States of America, year 2018. Requests for permission any portion of this book or for further information please contact us at www.TheresaWilsonBooks.com or by writing author Theresa V. Wilson at P.O. Box 47182, Windsor Mill, MD 21244. Writers in the Marketplace™ a subsidiary of VMAssociates, Inc.

Designed By: Creative Development Studios | Cover Picture By: Sensay

PREFACE

This guide is for those of you who have ideas in your head, or on "sticky notes", but you have yet to form those ideas into sentences, so that your sentences become paragraphs, and your paragraphs become chapters that create the first fiction or non-fiction book, play, or song. Procrastination, family-life issues, career, and unexpected events can all play a role in delaying your ability to produce the work. Your writing productivity is predicated upon how well you delegate your time. The purpose of this book is to help you manage the events and challenges you'll inevitably face as a writer, and to accept the fact that to be a writer, YOU HAVE TO COMMIT TO ACTUALLY WRITING!!

Before you begin, eliminate preparation delays each time you sit down to write. Make sure you have the following writer's tools available: pen/pencil, pad, sticky notes, and an "idea envelope" –which is a convenient place to store those "light bulb" ideas you can use later. Next, take a moment to remove anything that might interrupt your writing session. Deliberately position yourself in a secluded area, away from the noise. Mute your cell phone or, better yet, place it in another room.

Focus on family partnership. Remind them you are taking time, even if only for an hour, to review your work or write; initiate an agreement with your kids that includes a rewards system for them to work and play quietly while you spend time on your creative writing task. If you reinforce this habit with consistency, family and friends will eventually respect your schedule and work with you.

By choosing this book, you have opened a door to a unique opportunity. Get ready for an adventure that will help awaken the creativity *inside of you*, so its radiance shines on the paper *in front of you*.

- Prepare to remove fear, doubt and anxiety
- Be Determined to Shake yourself! Open your mind!
- Decide there are no more delays or hesitation
- Affirm to actively let go and move forward

ARE YOU READY TO EXPLODE ON THE SCENE?

"It doesn't matter what you want to write. It does matter that you decide to write."

Author Unknown

WRITING

According to Webster's Dictionary, writing is the act or
art of forming visible letters or characters that
serve as visible signs of ideas, words or symbols; or
a letter, note, or notice used to communicate or record.

Writing: A style or form of composition.
A Writer is:
Somebody who writes as a profession
Somebody who writes books or articles professionally
Someone who can write
Somebody who can write, who writes well, or
who enjoys writing." (Encarter World English Dictionary)

"Writing evolves in response to an issue, incident,
or revelation, usually centered on a personal experience.
-Theresa V. Wilson

Foreword

W. Terry Whalin
Author and Acquisitions Editor

I have always loved books because books change lives, and this book is a tremendous resource. For the last thirty years, I've been in publishing in different roles. I've written more than 60 books for traditional publishers. I've been a literary agent for a season and worked at three different publishers as an acquiring editor. Over the years I've worked with hundreds of authors. I've also written for more than 50 print magazines. People wonder, "How do you do all of this writing?"

It is not that I'm the best writer in the room but I am one of the most persistent. For years I've gone to writer's conferences and met editors. Like other writers, I pitch my ideas at the conference, then I listen for their feedback. When they express interest saying, "That's a good idea, Terry. Write that up and send it to me." I make a little note, then I go home and send it to the editor. It's not that each of my submissions get accepted or published—but they do get considered and into the process.

Now as an editor, I go to conferences, listen to writers' pitches and encourage them to send me their manuscript or proposal. Here's the reality, if you follow through and send the requested material, you are in the top 10% of writers at the event because many people never send in their material. They never follow through with the opportunity to get published and discover success.

Yes there are methods to getting your material into the expected format for a book proposal or a query letter or a pitch. Each of us can learn the format but the persistence and follow-through is something every writer can do.

You hold in your hands a valuable tool in this process. The Writer's Guide to Achieving Success: A Work book for Implementing the Plan contains detailed tools to help you in this process. There is no way around this truth: publishing is hard work. No little elves come out at night and magically produce stories or sentences on my computer. Writing on a regular basis is a discipline yet it's something each of us can learn and this book provides strategies to help you develop that discipline.

As you read through the pages of The Writer's Guide to Achieving Success, I encourage you to read deeply then apply the lessons to your own writing. Next get you material into the market and follow-through. There is a world of opportunity out there for each of us. Best wishes in your writing life.

W. Terry Whalin
Acquisitions Editor at Morgan James Publishing
www.straighttalkeditor.com

"Very little is written based purely on objective motives or observations. Writing is grounded in subjective emotional views, spiritual beliefs and opinions of the author."
-*Theresa V. Wilson*

THIS IS YOUR TIME TO EVOLVE, EXPERIENCE, AND CREATE.

OWNING YOUR WORK

This writer's workbook belongs to:

_____

Date

_____

TABLE OF CONTENTS

	Introduction	10
	It Begins with You: The Writer's Self-Assessment	13
Chapter 1	Writing Your Vision and Making it Clear	17-26
Chapter 2	Positive Outcomes of Building a "Deliberate" Relationship with Self	27-30
Chapter 3	Overcoming Pitfalls, Moving into Action	31-36
Chapter 4	Gaining a Sense of Purpose	37-42
Chapter 5	Tools, Tips, and Strategies for New Writers	43-48
Chapter 6	Moving Out of Neutral: The 500 Word Freedom Write	49-56
Chapter 7	Writing Critique Groups	57-60
Chapter 8	How to Submit Work for Publication	61-70
Chapter 9	Better is One Day: Taking Advantage of Writer Conferences	71-78
Chapter 10	Freelance Writers: Working from Home Is a Family Affair	79-82
Chapter 11	Dispelling the Myth about Self-Publishing	83-90
Chapter 12	Developing a Social Media Presence	91-98
Chapter 13	Expanding Your Market: Creating An Audiobook	99-102
Chapter 14	Creating "Your" Writer's Vision Board	103-106
	Glossary, Resources, and Conference Information	107-113
	Frequently Asked Questions	114-115

INTRODUCTION

CREATIVITY IN ACTION!

This is a "learn-by-doing" work book, providing an opportunity to choose various writing strategies you select, complete, and own. The learning material is structured to guide you through a systematic process that allows you to fully comprehend and embrace what it takes to produce quality writing. Success will depend on your willingness to let go of what you think you know about writing, and to be open to unique writing strategies designed to set you apart from other writers.

- It is time to let go; stop hesitating and doubting your abilities.
- It is time to lean on your inner Source for all knowledge.
- It is time to unlock your mind and allow your writing to flow from the depth of your being. If you do, your message will make a far greater impact on your readers.

The Writer's Guide to Achieving Success: A Workbook for Implementing the Plan provides a unique opportunity to explore, in detail, the world of writing. You are in the driver's seat! Each chapter includes practical suggestions and strategies that help you center, focus, and identify a suitable course of action leading to a completed work. Given the action steps, you must decide the time is **NOW** to make it happen.

EMBRACE YOUR STRENGTHS AND OVERCOME YOUR WEAKNESSES

The goal for The Writer's Guide to Success: A Workbook for Implementing the Plan is to create an urgency to accept the "call to action". It's a guide for transforming your thinking and changing your writing approach.

Starting with the concept of self-identification through self-assessment, you will:
- Identify your individual and unique challenges when writing
- Clarify your purpose for writing

- Develop a vision, a mission, and writing goals
- Practice effective strategies that will help you transition from the position of spectator to a producer of quality literary work.
- Complete exercises that help to identify your strengths, help define your genre, and address areas of challenge.

THINK BEYOND THE "QUICK FIX"

The Writer's Guide to Achieving Success: A workbook for Implementing the Plan, is not a "quick fix" instruction handbook—there are no shortcuts to writing. This is a workbook that offers a progression of steps including practice drills, insight on managing personal expectations, exploring writing opportunities, encouraging self-discipline, time management and commitment conducive to a writer's growth and development. The techniques recommended in this workbook will require self-discipline and determination which will result in your achieving your best work.

Like a musician with his instrument, aspiring writers must practice, review, critique, edit, refine, and implement consistent writing techniques. In the end, your words will come alive, provoking readers to move to action. They will react, reflect, or respond because of something you were able to create.

Are you ready to influence, improve, and impact the lives of your readers? There's no better time to begin than right now.

The chart on the next page is a sample of the "writing experience" cycle. We each have unique additions to this cycle, depending on the choices we make. However, the basic process remains the same.

- You will begin with an idea leading to some form of research or investigation.
- You will write, rewrite, edit, and write again and again.
- You will attend conferences and create a personal brand.
- You will seek ways to market and promote your ideas to editors, publishers, and endorsers.

The Writing Experience

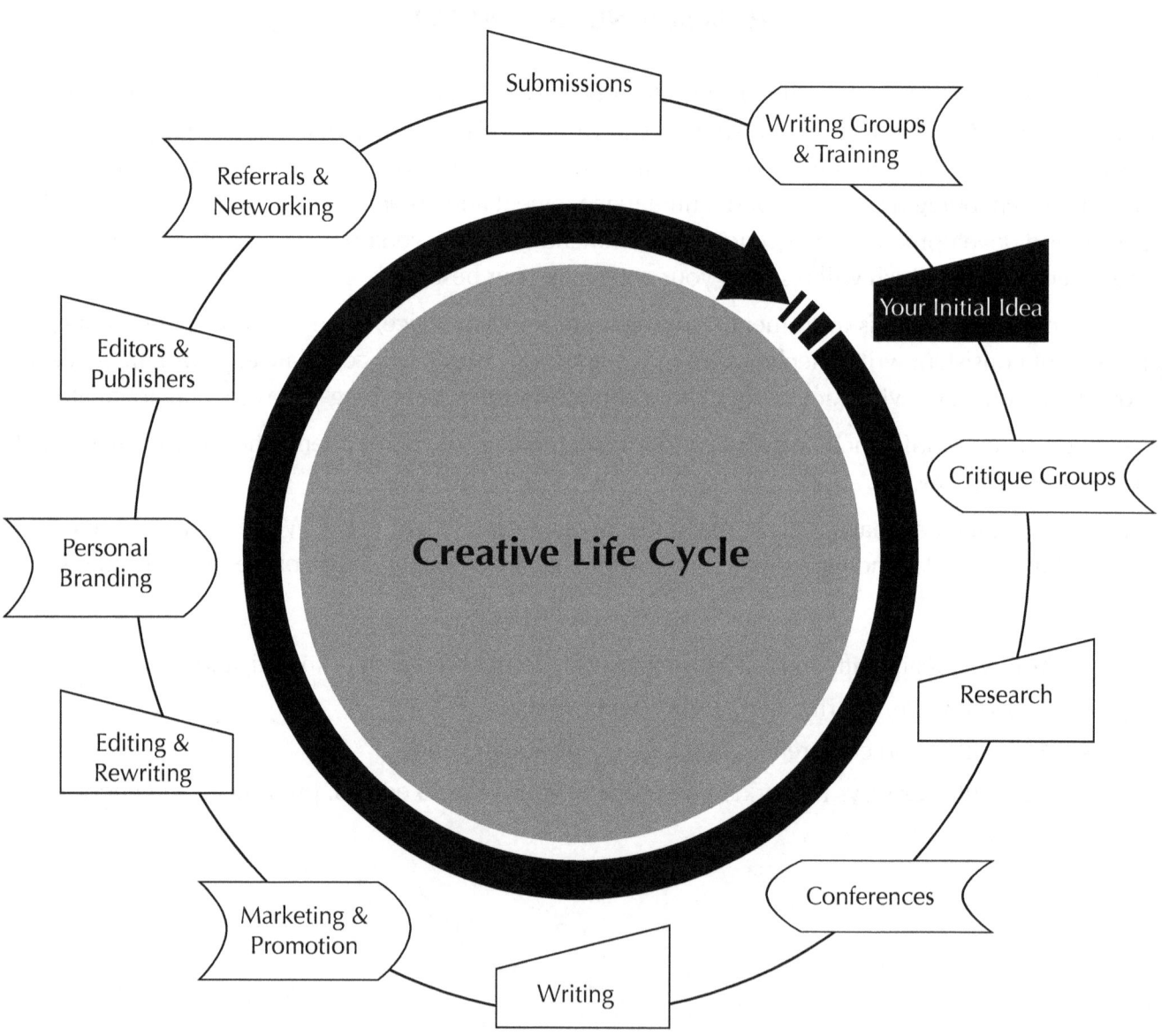

IT ALL BEGINS WITH YOU

Challenges to Getting Started: Self Assessment Worksheet ©2009

Writers should be able to detect personal behaviors and environmental issues (including people) that may affect their ability to initiate a writing project. The following exercise will help you detect actual and potential inhibitors to getting started.

Directions: Write whatever issue you feel inhibits your starting, or continuing, process of writing, listing number one (1) as your greatest level of concern and number six (6) as your least level of concern.

*What is the Issue?	Level of Concern					
	1	2	3	4	5	6
1.						
2.						
3.						
4.						
5.						
6.						
7.						
8.						
9.						
10.						
11.						
12.						
13.						
14.						
15.						

Use one word or phrase to describe issue

Getting Ready: Creating Your Author's Space

Not unlike an artist's studio, writers need to identify a space that will generate the atmosphere that will encourage writing. Pick a place where you can leave your materials (journals, pens, paper, post its, etc.) at all times. It should be away from the general "living space" of your home to eliminate potential to procrastinate or delay getting started. Create this space now so that you can make this workbook the first item accessible your writer's space. Here are some quick, easy steps:

1. Clean the area (vacuum, sweep, and remove dust). By "cleaning" your space, you create a mental picture of a 'fresh start'.
2. Burn a candle or use a diffuser with fragrance oils to set a stress free atmosphere conducive for clarity when writing.
3. Clear the clutter: remove all unrelated materials (unrelated books and magazines, papers).
4. Keep your favorite materials handy (pens, pencils, pads, journals, paper clips, post it notes, etc.). Do this so that once you enter your space, you aren't delayed by having to leave the area to search for items that should be readily available at all times.

CHAPTER 1

WRITING YOUR VISION MAKING IT CLEAR

A writer is truly a word artist whose canvas is a sheet of paper. Your words can bring hope, joy, laughter and support.

The first step to achieving writing success is accepting the fact that you are the common denominator for your ultimate success or failure. It is a personal choice as to whether you move forward or remain in the state of "permanent potential". The second step is identifying your audience. The third step is possessing a clear "vision" of what you want to communicate through your writing.

'Vision statements' focus on the future and address the following questions: What impact do I want my writing to have on others? Where do I see my writing in 3 to 5 years? How will I reach my audience? Your writer's vision statement sets the tone for what you will write, defines the future path you'll take with writing choices, and provides direction for your writing. Your vision statement is also an expression of your personal desire for the direction of your writing. As you draft your vision statement, make sure you address the following questions:

- What do you desire to achieve by your writing? What is really on your heart to communicate to others?
- What will be different about your life once you've achieved your writing goal?
- How will you feel once the book is published?
- Who do you want to impact with your message and why?
- Is writing a novel the best medium to make your point? If not, what other writing form could you use?

Your vision statement formulates out of your heart's desire for something to happen. It is the center of who you are, how you view and respond to situations, and how you want to be viewed in relation to others.

Your writer's vision statement will describe how you see yourself in relation to the world. It is a way of defining how you want to influence those who will read your work. (It is always important to begin any endeavor by assessing the status of where you are and how you perceive your strengths and weaknesses.) This strategy will help lay the foundation for identifying what, if any, preliminary steps needed to ensure positive results with your writing. There are several steps to this process.

Step I: The following strengths assessment exercise will help you address issues as you prepare for writing your best work. The 1st form provides space to list what might be your ultimate accomplishments as a writer. The next form is to outline writing weaknesses (example: Procrastination). The last box is to list strategies for improvement. On this form, prepare a list of specific resources needed to successfully move forward.

POSSIBILITIES TO POTENTIAL ASSESSMENT

In this box list what might be your ultimate accomplishments as a writer:

In this box list any writing weaknesses in which you're already aware:

> In this box prepare a list of specific resources or strategies you can use to address the identified writing weaknesses:

Step 2: Analyzing Incomplete Work

Take a moment to think about work you have not completed. It's important, as you move forward, to assess the chief reasons for incompletion of other projects and determine what you could have done differently. This helps to ensure any new, writing projects reaching their completion, without the same challenges. Write responses to the following:

<u>Main reasons for not completing the work:</u>

1._____
2._____
3._____

<u>Strategies to address the reasons for incomplete work:</u>

1._____
2._____
3._____

Everyone's vision is different. We all can look at the same thing and reach different opinions and perspectives. This is what makes writing fun! Let's start the process of preparing your **Writer's Vision Statement.** First, let's discover who you are and your preferences. Use the form below to highlight activities you enjoy and comment on how they make you feel.

DETAILING YOUR GOALS:

The following exercise provides an outline designed to encourage you to identify and prioritize interests, and to decide which subjects-areas to address when detailing your writing goals. This exercise may also help to provide a focal point for your writing genre. In order to create a Vision, you will need to list goals. Your mission is the destination; your goals are guideposts along the path to your destination.

In developing your Vision statement, you should consider your ultimate goals. These goals should state the outcomes of what you'd expect to accomplish, and will inadvertently answer questions gained from the writing experience. There should be at least 3-5 goals for each area or topic addressed in your vision statement. Remember, your goals are the driving force behind your vision statement.

1. List three things you are interested in accomplishing within the next: **3 Months:**

_____
_____
_____
_____

6 Months:

_____
_____
_____
_____

12 Months:

_____
_____
_____
_____

2. Are there any issues that may prevent your accomplishment of the goals outlined above?

_____
_____
_____
_____

PREPARING OBJECTIVES

Many people waste valuable time because they lack clear objectives. They proceed through life diligentlyworking on several projects, never developing a clear picture of what they are striving to accomplish. Lack of clarity in your objectives can create conflict in the choices you make and conclusions reached. Having defined objectives provides help in maintaining your writing's focal point, and a timeline of how long it will take to reach the destination.

Objectives are details of what it will take to reach the stated goals. To prevent conflict, your objectives should be specific, measurable, attainable, results-focused, and time-bound with details that, when followed, connect you to the desired result. Remember, your objectives should state what's needed to meet a desired outcome, and they should include any needed specific tasks to meet the desired goal.

For each of the goals listed in the exercise above, write their specific objectives. For example, a six-month goal may be to complete an unfinished manuscript. My objectives for completing this goal would include the following:

(a) Actively devoting a portion of the day towards quiet time "journal writing".

(b) Deliberately setting aside two hours per day for researching, reading, and/or collecting data about the topic of interest.

(c) Purposefully writing 2-3 pages three times per week until project completion. I am a morning person, so my most productive writing hours are early a.m.

(d) Visually exploring creative ideas by visiting museums, walking in the park, observing events, or doing whatever encourages creative thinking.

(e) Consciously limiting television and radio time. For 21 days, I challenge you to follow scheduled hours for viewing television programs and/or listening to the radio. Studies show that an action becomes a habit after 21 days.

Assignment: Use the Goals Planning Worksheet on the next page to help outline the details for meeting specific goals and objectives.

Visual "mapping" is important for monitoring progress. The following form is a helpful tool measure your progress toward meeting the specific goals outlined above.

SELF-ASSESSMENT EXERCISE: COMPLETING THE WRITING VISION STATEMENT

One step, as part of the writer's transition process, is initiating action steps leading to a completed vision for your writing. The process is simple, but it begins with specific actions you must complete. Answers to the following questions will help you begin the process. There are no limits to where these statements may finally lead. As you consider your responses, be honest with yourself. Most importantly, Establish a Set Time to Write.

THE WRITERS GUIDE

Goal #1	SPECIFIC STEPS FOR MEETING GOAL	TIMELINE (Days) 10 30 60 Other
	_____ _____ _____ _____	Why will it take this long?

Goal #2		
	_____ _____ _____ _____	Why will it take this long?

Goal #3		
	_____ _____ _____ _____	Why will it take this long?

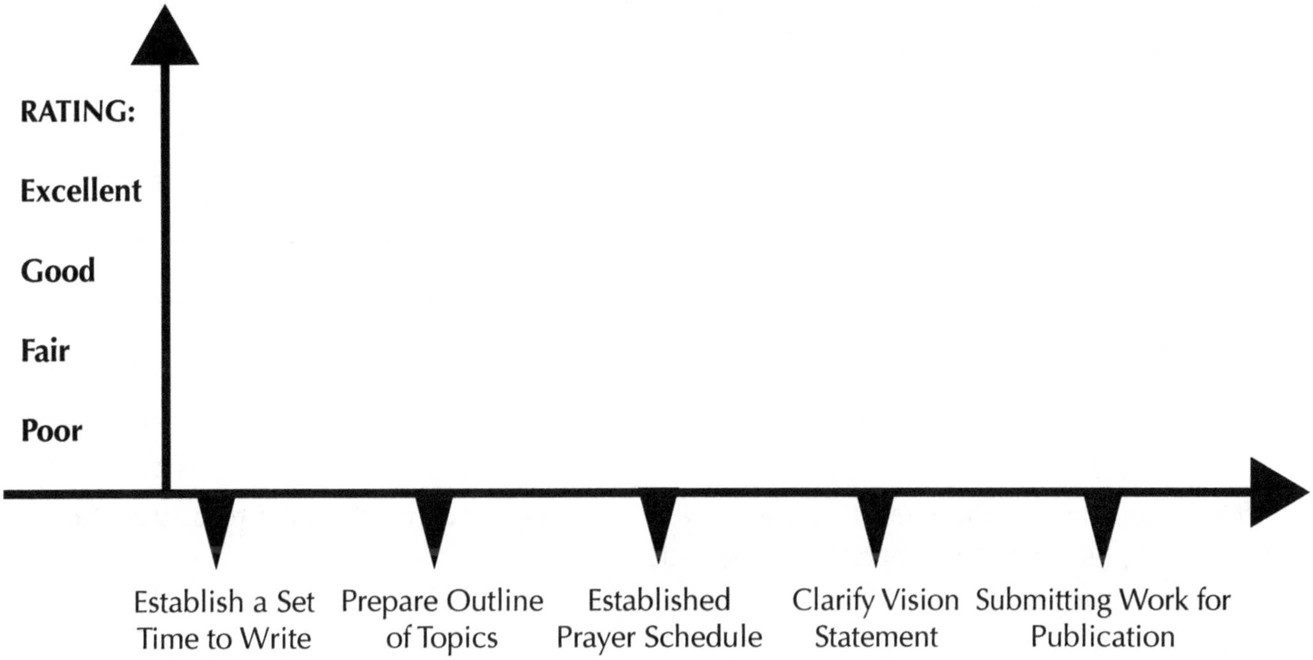

Writing Your Vision, "Making It Clear" | 23

```
RATING:

Excellent

Good

Fair

Poor
```

Establish a Set   Prepare Outline   Established   Clarify Vision   Submitting Work for
Time to Write   of Topics   Prayer Schedule   Statement   Publication

```
RATING:     (Your Copy)

Excellent

Good

Fair

Poor
```

1. What do you spend most of your free time doing? Why?

2. If you suddenly discovered you inherited more money than you would ever need, how would you spend your time?

3. If you could live anywhere in the world, where would it be?

4. Have you ever kept a diary or journal? If yes, what kinds of subjects, topics did you write?

5. What do you feel is the most important accomplishment of your life thus far?

6. What do you feel would make your life more successful?

7. Write down five important points that you would want others to know about you:

_____

_____

_____

_____

_____

After completing the above exercise, review your answers and connect similar responses. Now, look at the phrases and ask yourself these questions:

(a) Will any of these phrases or statements contribute to specific aspects of what you want to convey in your writing?

(b) What emotional areas will they address?

(c) How useful, educational, motivational and/or practical will your written work be to others?

When the reader elects to review your information, they need to see value in it for themselves. Your Writer's vision statement should address the benefit(s) achieved by reading your work, as well as include the consideration of the answers to the questions above.

Using a separate sheet of paper, imagine five years from now speaking to a group of people who are asking about your vision for writing. Your response should be specific in describing aspects of your writing you believe make it unique and successful. It can also include any themes of focus of which you were passionate about during that those years.

The following page includes an example of a vision statement:

VISION STATEMENT EXAMPLE
Theresa V. Wilson, M.Ed., CPBA | WRITERSINTHEMARKETPLACE©

"Writers in the Marketplace is a coaching resource and training firm that rises above the ordinary by creating and delivering messages that influence transformation in the lives of writers. It also helps them to accomplish what they have been inspired to do. It provides strategies that motivate people to recognize and develop their empowerment to accomplish anything they desire. Writers in the Marketplace provides programs that successfully help writers reach their full potential, resulting in enhanced spiritual and mental capacities to produce quality writing, ultimately leading to a published work."

Now it's Your Turn: Write Your Vision

_____
_____
_____
_____
_____
_____
_____
_____
_____

ESTABLISHING YOUR WRITING MISSION STATEMENT

Remember, the Vision Statement is usually broad, lengthy, and can include "global" planning: "To reach the world with helpful strategies that moves them in the direction of self- empowerment in the areas of_____." (It is for your eyes only)

Your Mission Statement, however, is shorter, more focused, and direct. It will proclaim who you are, what you offer, the genre of your writing, and convey the meaning of your writing to those who take the time to explore the contents. It should be clear and specific. It will be part of your "brand," seen by the public. Some writers will have their mission statements printed on the back of their business cards.

Here is one example:

Wal-Mart – "To give ordinary folk the chance to buy the same thing as rich people."

Mary Kay Cosmetics – "To give unlimited opportunity to women."

CHAPTER 2

POSITIVE OUTCOMES OF BUILDING A "DELIBRATE RELATIONSHIP WITH SELF:

ESTABLISH A PATTERN OF COMPLETED WORK

There is power in developing deliberate relationships. According to international speaker Dr. Roger P. Levin, DDS, CEO of The Levin Group, "Deliberate relationships are typically what occur in the business world. Both individuals involved in deliberate relationships are motivated by self-interest. The ultimate-question is, "How is this relationship going to benefit me and my business?" In business, the emphasis is building a consistent, positive level of interaction. The ultimate goal of developing and maintaining a long term "deliberate" relationship, resulting in a beneficial return on the investment, is so that the self-interest of all can be met.

The above description is the typical "best business practice". If implemented on a regular basis, successful relationships are guaranteed, resulting in repeat business and accelerated client referrals. Let's consider the outcome of using these techniques to develop and strengthen our "deliberate" connection with our inner selves? In these next pages, we will view several successful "sales" relationship strategies used to improve customer/client relations, along with spiritual self-reflection practices that may, when used consistently, enhance your ability to connect with your internal courage.

Sales Relationship #1 Establishing Rapport

According to leading experts, during the "qualifying phase" of the selling process, the salesperson can greatly benefit from utilizing strategies that enable them to delve deeper into the relationship. This contributes to the success of the client/customer relationship. It is this deliberate relationship-building process that enables them to get an end product, resulting in clearer directions and tasks necessary for success. Salespeople are required to use their investigative strategies to learn the answers to the following questions: Who is the key decision maker? What is the organizational structure? What does it take to connect? How are decisions made? What are the possible dangers to success?

What is the value of establishing positive outcomes? What strengths does the salesperson bring to the relationship? The result of all these tactics is the foundation for the establishment of genuine rapport with the customer leading to a sale.

Connecting with Self

By applying the "Establishing sales rapport" principles outlined above, the transformation that can take place, when deliberately exploring the inner self, can be amazing. The process though not complicated requires consistency and a sincere desire to discover what motivates you to action. The tools most useful in accomplishing this level of personal awareness should include completing a personal inventory assessment, which can help you identify writing interests. Once inventories are completed, the atmosphere is then ripe for change and redesigning, so you can implement new strategies that increase your potential to succeed with your writing goals.

Learning more about your target Audience

Sales people spend a great deal of their time gathering information about their prospects. Any number of reports is available using the internet (Dun & Brad Street) and other business databases.

Depending on the product or service, sales people will have accessibility to other professionals and their previous customers. They'll get to ask questions of other salespersons, vendors, and representatives who've had direct business relations with the individual customer. The purpose of these strategies is to enable salespersons to gain insight about the prospect that aids in planning the appropriate responses to needs, provides appropriate reactions to objections, coaches them through a process, and/or presents solutions they can follow. Learning more about the customer (potential reader) enhances the salesperson's ability to respond with more confidence and knowledge, thereby demonstrating expertise in meeting their needs or writing interests.

The Listening Room Experience

We need to make room in our daily living to spend time in our "listening room". Establishing a pattern of being still, listening to music, and relaxing your mind is a great method for clearing the mental clutter of the day's activities. Here are several suggested guidelines to help you start with this process:

(1) Schedule "quiet time" on a daily basis. Commit to the schedule you chose.

(2) Clear the noise clutter and reduce distractions (i.e. radio, television, telephone, Facebook and other social media). Inform your family and friends of your appointment, and ask not to be disturbed during this designated time.

(3) Take a pen/pencil and writing pad, so you can note any ideas or feelings you may want to review later.

(4) Take a few moments to play inspirational music, which potentially creates an atmosphere con-

ducive for creativity. Remember, your goal is to work toward spending quiet, reflective time and journaling your thoughts.

(5) Commit to doing all the above consecutively for 21 days;

Presenting the Product Using the WOW Factor

In business, knowing your product is only half the battle. Presenting the product is what ultimately creates the sale. Though Pillsbury and Duncan Hines use the same ingredients to make their cake mix, each spends millions of dollars per year on marketing ads, promotions, and materials that make their products unique, and highly presentable and acceptable to the consumer. Every sales strategy is created and implemented using a special combination unique to their particular product. Their company goal is to increase sales by demonstrating that their product is "the one" that will meet the needs of the consumer.

Writers must also be enthusiastic about the product they're creating, so that potential customers become interested and purchase with confidence. As writers grow more knowledgeable about their writing topic, consistently follow through with their theme and concept, and develop confidence in speech and rapport with others, they will have inadvertently created the WOW factor in writing.

CHAPTER 3

OVERCOMING PITFALLS, MOVING INTO ACTION

Writers WRITE!! This is a simple, but conclusive fact. You can lose momentum when you delay putting pen to paper or when you allow interruptions to sidetrack your efforts. There are techniques that help avoid the non-action pitfalls to writing, but none of them will override the brutal fact that writers control their actions that lead to the end result—a completed written work ready for publication. Your delay in completing a work could negatively affect the spiritual growth and development for some of your potential readers, and their encouragement and progression of transitioning to a greater level may be stunted.

Addressing time-management, repelling interruptions, and practicing when to say "no" are the three crucial techniques that can propel the writer towards action. Readiness to write can take many forms. For some, it is a discovery of the impact their writing has on others via short stories, newsletters, special occasion narratives, poetry, and/or speeches. For others, there is an awareness of responses to messages they prepared when assigned to initiate a project or program.

The urge or "unction" for writing is an innate skill and gift. It is an inner prompting or need that creates an urgency to express, in writing, the emotions, aspirations, and inspiration that emerge from the depth of your very being. For most writers, writing readiness is the urge to put mental pictures on paper.

Writers never have to be told who they are. The urgency in their creative spirit speaks for itself. The inability to create on paper the inner thoughts of one's mind is indescribable. A call to write is clear. Accepting and pursuing that call is where most of us fail.

How to Accept Responsibility

Writing is a choice. You are the catalyst for the results you seek. By following several simple strategies on a consistent basis, you can mature in the call on your life:

1 Establish a time to write and begin on time (no matter how many agenda items appear to clutter your day). Consistently beginning your writing on time sends a message to your "inner self" and others around you of the seriousness of your commitment.

2. Have a prepared agenda outlined. It is important to have a beginning and an end to your identified writing process, so that you're encouraged to organize your thoughts in the same manner.

3. Make "Inner Refresh" a number one (#1) agenda item. Be aware that the real Person in charge of your writing time is the Holy Spirit Who will guide your process. Praying and seeking God's face early in the day will net great results during your writing time. The reward of sacrifice is knowing that Father never disappoints us. He knows what we need before we ask. Time with the Lord can only result in "gold nuggets" that can be shared by all.

4. Keep the agenda. Write the vision... make it plain. A rambling agenda encourages rambling thoughts, leading to disorganized writing. You may have to "shelf" other ideas to ensure that the present agenda completes.

5. Include time for assessment of any progress, problems, and accomplishments. Underscore important issues that require further attention, but be mindful not to stray from the task. A To-Do list is a great resource in this area. Jotting down plans to address an issue relieves anxiety and pressure to respond immediately.

6. Highlight successes at the end of your writing time. Review what you've accomplished. Family members and friends are great sources of support and encouragement. Seek their opinions—give way to constructive criticism. Even if it is only a chapter, celebrate all movements that get you closer to the other side—completion. You also create personal credibility in acknowledging stages of success, demonstrating the capacity for a final product.

7. Provide follow-up assignments that include concrete, measurable objectives to be met in preparation for the next writing session. A readiness to report at least one completed step in the progression of accomplishments is beneficial.

8. Ask for input from a family member when preparing "action steps". Writers have no excuse for not writing. Accountability partners are very helpful resources for maintaining goals. Their role is crucial to helping you analyze personal goal progression, recommend steps to take to avoid stagnation. . This interactive practice encourages you to face the issue and make a decision to move forward.

9. Establish a buddy system. This is highly recommended. We all need someone who will confront us, inquiring why we have not written a paragraph or completed a project. As a team, you can each suggest and develop strategies to address the challenges you face individually. A great resource for this strategy is joining a writers group.

Writing Your Vision, "Making It Clear" | 33

As writers, the most difficult step while transitioning from information to implementation of action is taking the first step—just do it! If you are steadfast and immoveable in meeting your writing goals, and are faithful to follow the strategies, you will reap immeasurable benefits.

IDENTIFYING WHO I AM AND WHAT I LIKE

On the lines below, list four activities you like to do, then use the list and circle the words that describe how each activity makes you feel (i.e. energized, warm, silly, etc.):

ACTIVITIES I REALLY ENJOY

_____

_____

_____

ACTIVITIES I DON'T ENJOY

_____

_____

_____

What topics would you like to write about? Why?

_____

_____

_____

_____

Words that Describe How I Feel:	
Pleasant	Playful
Excited	Nice
Warm	Peaceful
Forgiving	Friendly
Energized	Fun
Pleased	Confident
Happy	Content
Joyful	Cheerful
Generous	Grateful
Silly	Hopeful
Positive	Focused
Capable	Restful
Discouraged	Angry
Anxious	Sad
Annoyed	Agitated
Scared	Restless
Fearful	Unhappy
Grouchy	Unsure
Irritated	Negative
Hostile	Lonely
Frustrated	Aggressive
Uneasy	Phony

Assignment:

After observing each of the next five pictures, write 250 words, or more, that describe your general thoughts about the pictures and the feelings you feel while viewing each one. **Note:** Your writing can be in the form of poetry, a short story, a song, or a play. You're the author, you decide.

34 | THE WRITERS GUIDE

Give Your Writing a Title

_____
_____
_____
_____

_____
_____
_____
_____

Give Your Writing a Title

_____
_____
_____
_____

_____
_____
_____
_____

Give Your Writing a Title

_____
_____
_____
_____

_____
_____
_____
_____

Writing Your Vision, "Making It Clear" | 35

Give Your Writing a Title

_____
_____
_____
_____
_____
_____
_____
_____

Give Your Writing a Title

_____
_____
_____
_____
_____
_____
_____
_____

Quick Reminders

- You will not always be assigned a writing project; sometimes you will have to create it or discover it.
- You must be self-directed and self-disciplined to write.
- You must fight distractions and mood swings.
- You must remain self-motivated to be successful.
- You must make writing a top priority.
- You must remain faithful to your goals and to the strategies that support those goals.
- You must maintain positive self-talk
- You must devote time towards prayer and meditation in your "listening room".

**"There is one thing stronger than all the armies in the world
And that is an idea whose time has come."
-Victor Hugo**

CHAPTER 4

GAINING A SENSE OF PURPOSE

   Determining the purpose and plan for your writing is no different than the steps used determining the purpose and plan for your career, or life. Observing, listening, reading, and testing are common steps to finding what influences our life's decisions.

   For those of us with a spiritual foundation, we lean on the knowledge and understanding of who we are and what we know inwardly about ourselves. Whatever you choose to listen to determine the outcome of your actions and reflects in your writing. Whatever choice you make will confirm the path (purpose) you've chosen. Always consider asking, "What do I want others to see?" "How do I want to be remembered?"

"<u>Assignment</u>: "Assessing Your Purpose".
Write responses to the following questions:

1. What aspects of writing give you the greatest satisfaction?

_____
_____
_____
_____

2. What do you like least about writing?

_____
_____

THE WRITERS GUIDE

_____

3. Describe the environment that provokes your best writing.

_____
_____
_____
_____

4. What is absent when you are at your best while writing?

_____
_____
_____
_____

5. Do you know what you have been "called" to write? ( ) Yes ( ) No. If yes, please explain:

_____
_____
_____
_____

6. If you could afford to devote your life to serving others, what would you do?

_____
_____
_____
_____

Here are several suggested guidelines to help you begin the writing process:

    (a) **Consistency and Commitment.** Consistently devote yourself to quiet time; commit to this time on a daily or weekly basis.

    (b) **Clear the noise and clutter.** Reduce the distractions (radio, television, telephone, internet, etc.). Inform your family and friends that you have an appointment and are not to be disturbed during this specified time. Note: It may be necessary to disconnect the phone during this time.

(c) ***Take a pen/pencil and writing pad*** into your listening area to record any ideas or feelings you may want to review later.

(d) ***Have a cassette recorder/DVD player*** available for inspirational music that will help set-the atmosphere for praise and worship. Remember, however, your goal is to work towards spending quiet, reflective time listening for His voice. Note: Limiting the use of music may help.

(e) ***Inspirational resources.*** Have the Bible accessible, along with any other inspirational materials. Oftentimes, reading a scripture verse or two will center you on the Lord.

Make a commitment to do this exercise for 21 days. Don't quit!

The following time management assessment charts are designed to help you identify your lifestyle choices, as well as potential times for listening and writing. The first chart provides a list of specific times and recommends color-coding strategies. On the second chart, you may write summary activities with specific start and end times. You can also assess whether the activity was productive or wasteful.

The final exercise will help you assess results to determine where you've positioned your priorities.

WRITING AND TIME MANAGEMENT CHOICES

You've spent 21 days monitoring your activities. You now have an idea of how you spend your time. Write three things you would do if you had an extra hour each day.

1. _____
2. _____
3. _____

Look at your responses. Now, write one comment (per item) about what you can and cannot control, as it relates to the choices made in #1 and #3.

Example: #1 might be the choice to complete writing a chapter in your book

I have Total control over	**I have No Control over**
Whether I choose to answer the phone or acknowledge a text message.	Getting children from school at 3:30p.m.

THE WRITERS GUIDE

Your Items:
   #1 _____   _____
   #2 _____   _____
   #3 _____   _____

Mastery of time management, according to Franklin Covey's Time Quest, involves the ability to master our control over personal events. We have the same number of hours per day. Our challenges lie in our choices to take charge over those things we can control, believing we can make the necessary adjustments to improve the course of events in our day.

Helpful forms: The following form will help you monitor daily activities and detect "time wasters". Make 21 copies of this form. Write your activities (phone, dinner, shopping, writing, etc.) per day.

Identifying Time Wasters

Weekday _____ Your Name _____

Time	Activity		Comments
8:00			
9:00			
10:00			
11:00			
12:00			
1:00			
2:00			
3:00			
4:00			
5:00			
6:00			
7:00			
8:00			

Monitor your routine for 10 days. Use Codes for repeated Activities (e.g. Dinner = "D", Breakfast = "BF", or Workday = "WD", Telephone = "Tele", Writing = "WR")

ANALYZING WRITING AND TIME MANAGEMENT CHOICES

Once you've completed 21 days of monitoring your activities, you will have a better idea of how you spend your time.

Write five things you would do if you had an extra hour each day:

1. _____
2. _____
3. _____
4. _____
5. _____

Rank your responses above using 1-5: 1 = greatest priority, 5 = lowest priority. Using the above responses, write 2-3 things you can do to create that extra hour for your greatest priority:

1. _____
2. _____
3. _____

CHAPTER 5

TOOLS, TIPS, and STRATEGIES FOR NEW WRITERS

Determining your writing interest

To achieve any level of success in writing, it is important to start and maintain a clear focus on who you are and what you intend to represent through your writing. No matter the subject, writers possess a writing style used to communicate with their audience. Generally, they describe a response to personal experiences, observations, attitudes, and behaviors.

Choosing from topics, such as home-life, work, relationships, etc. can prove challenging, making even seasoned writers struggle to maintain focus on any one specific topic at a time. For new writers, this can be extremely challenging. It is essential to identify how and when you developed an interest or passion for any one-subject area. Before you begin the following exercise, find a place void of distractions. You are beginning a journey. Your destination point is to get your literary work published.

Assignment: Part A

The following exercise provides questions that encourages a heightened awareness of your most dsired interests. After completing the survey, you'll discover a focal point for your writing. Answer the questions with as much detail as possible. Have fun with it! Let your mind wander.

1. If you had no restrictions, what would you spend most of your free time doing? Why?

_____
_____
_____

2. If you inherited more money than you would ever need, what would you spend your time doing?
_____
_____
_____
_____

3. If you could live anywhere in the world, where would it be? Why? _____
_____
_____
_____
_____

4. List three things you are interested in accomplishing within the next 6 months:
_____
_____
_____
_____

5. Have you ever maintained a diary or journal? If so, what were the most memorable topics? (e.g. summer vacations, dating experiences, family activities, etc.) _____
_____
_____
_____
_____

6. What do you feel is the most important accomplishment of your life thus far?
_____
_____
_____

7. List five important things you would want others to know about you and/or your family:

_____
_____
_____
_____
_____

Assignment: Part B

After completing the above exercise, review your statements. Group related responses. For example, in #6 you were asked to list your most important accomplishments.

Your response to this item may be similar to one of the items listed in item #7 or item #1 and item #4 may have similar responses.

Assignment: Part C "Focusing on a Topic to Write About"

Pick one of the groupings in Part B. Write two (2) paragraphs that include information, descriptions of the topic or situation.

_____
_____
_____
_____
_____
_____
_____
_____
_____
_____
_____
_____
_____
_____
_____
_____

Why are you interested in writing?

Most writers are readers, first. They read extensively, whether it's historical, scientific research, romantic mystery, or inspirational literary works. Sometimes they've experienced challenges because of life-changing transitions, as well. Remember, your best writing already is in you.

Let's talk about how to write those thoughts on paper. First, take time to discover what inspires you:

Are You A Romantic? We all have that special someone—first love, new love, or unforgettable moments that strengthened a love relationship. Draw from those experiences and allow them to influence your writing.

Do You Love to Travel? Don't consider taking that next trip without a pad, pen, or tape recorder. Become aware of your surroundings, and "take in" the ambience and décor. Many magazine publishers would appreciate a first-hand description of popular vacation "hot spots" or cruise packages. It's a great way to "break the ice" and achieve your first byline.

Are You Interested in Healthy Eating? Canvas health and family magazines and review cuisine commentary pages of local newspapers. Your approach might include writing an overview of various uses of health foods, like Tofu. You also might include tasty recipe ideas, along with photographs of the final dish.

How About "How-To"? Have you ever wondered how books like "Computers for Idiots" became popular? Don't! Generally, people want to know how to do just about every conceivable thing. You may have skills in home improvement, gardening, and/or interior decorating "hacks". Whatever it is, someone wants to read it. All you need to do is write the details. As a first-time writer, focus upon what you know or have personally experienced. Let the words flow. Don't analyze your thoughts often. Spending too much time rethinking can spoil a great work in the making.

Stay personal. Write as if you are verbally telling the story or having a conversation with a good friend. Maintaining a casual attitude keeps you relaxed and open to ideas and witty thoughts. Let your first draft be a "free flowing" experience. Have fun with it. You can get technical later. Eventually it becomes a part of you. The more you write, the more you improve, and the more comfortable you'll become.

Writing Your Vision, "Making It Clear" | 47

The Place to Start:

- **Meditate.** Spend Quiet-Time/Meditate. Seek wisdom as you begin your writing project. While writing, set aside what you assume you know and just relax. Submit your mind to what you feel in your spirit. Trust your intuition.
- **Avoid Distractions.** Once you've made the commitment of time, stick to it, and don't let anything or anyone (barring emergencies) interfere until the allotted writing time is complete. Give the work your total attention for that designated time.
- **Read Inspirational Messages.** Let the information provide the peace, comfort, enlightenment, and encouragement needed to complete the task. Sometimes it is only a matter of reading one message multiple times, so that it becomes a part of your thinking—and maybe even your writing motto.
- **Listen to Music.** Let the music comfort and soothe you, as well as inspire your creativity.
- **Stay Positive.** Approach your writing with an attitude of expectation. Expect to produce a great work (poem, article, book, song, or play) that will bring joy and peace, educating and encouraging the reader.
- **Always Start with What You Know.** Personal experiences are powerful! We learn things in our everyday lives that contribute "how-to" narratives with lists and suggestions.
- **Keep a Writing Checklist**

It is helpful to create a checklist of questions to consider before writing:

1. Will anyone want to read this material? If so, why? _____
_____
_____

2. Am I knowledgeable about the topic or have I researched this subject sufficiently? If not, list the steps you'll take to make this happen? *(Ex: 1. I will go to the library or use the internet to search the topic. 2. I will interview people who are familiar with this subject. 3. I will take a course in this subject field.)*
_____
_____
_____

3. Do my thoughts flow well? Am I staying with, and fully developing my thoughts? ( ) Yes ( ) No
If no, what do you feel is missing? What resources or skilled persons could be of assistance to you?

_____
_____

4. Who, specifically, do I think would be interested in reading this work?

Age Range: _____ Gender: _____ Culture (if applicable) _____

Religion (if applicable) _____ Other: _____

5. Does my writing do one of the following?

    ___ generate an emotional response (pity, happiness, sadness, hope, anger, etc.)

    ___ provide inspiration (encouraging, supportive, enlightenment)

    ___ provoke a "call to action" (to do something different or dramatic, move forward, change attitude, accomplish/complete a task, etc.)

6. Is my message meaningful, life-changing, and memorable? ( ) Yes ( ) No

For who? _____

CHAPTER 6
MOVING OUT OF NEUTRAL:
THE 500 WORD FREEDOM WRITE

It happens to every writer at one point on another. You know you want to write but find you are more focused on sentence structure than content. Using correct grammar and structuring paragraphs to change thoughts are all part of writing. You will not get published without it. In the beginning, however, it is important to establish a "personal rhythm". One way to accomplish this is by "journaling."

To encourage journaling, I've created what I call the '500 Word Freedom Write'. I select a topic and "free- flow" write until I have exhausted everything I think even remotely relates to the subject. I may or may not use paragraph indentions. I spend quiet time meditating and using my intuition to develop witty thoughts about the topic and continue to write (or type) until I feel I've exhausted the idea. I do not edit or check spelling during this process, as it could break the flow of creativity and disconnect me from the Source of my inspiration. Focus is the ultimate aim, writing the ultimate goal. If you practice this method consistently, it will usually result in 500-700 words or more, depending on the subject.

Often, after I complete my "freedom write", I review the content for useful words, sentences, and/or phrases that may be used for other writing projects. At other times, I continue to develop the work until it either becomes an article or chapter of a book I'm planning to write. The beauty of the 500 Word Freedom Write process is that there's no pressure to do anything more than write. It is either based upon what you are currently feeling, something you read that inspired you, or a personal experience. This strategy can help you gain a clearer understanding of a topic. Many of my articles evolved from my Freedom Writing sessions.

The following journal page is a handy tool for the "500 Word Freedom Writing" sessions, called the Writing Gallery. This provides space for you to identify your writing moments sources. By completing this exercise consistently, you will be able to determine which Gallery moments have the greatest impact on your writing.

As a helpful strategy, use the following column descriptions to assist in completing the Writing Gallery Log on the next page. Remember, this is a "write without thinking" moment. For inspiration, you might decide to take a stroll along the beach or in the woods, or you may choose to spend time quietly reflecting at home. The key is to release and let the words flow on paper. Make a commitment to follow this guide once a day for 10 days. Consistency could result in completing your first article or a chapter in your next novel.

>**Column One** – identify the source of the Gallery moment (E) indicates an external environmental influence. (i.e. music, quote of the day, or sermon topic); (I) indicates your internal response of the external influence, past memories, and/or "witty inventions" from your spirit (inwardly).
>
>**Column Two** – briefly describe the situation, or event.
>
>**Column Three** – assess your physical reactions. (Ex: pain in your gut; feeling warm and tingly; sweaty palms, etc.)
>
>**Column Four** – describe your immediate thoughts during your gallery moment. Don't process or rethink the comment or idea... just write!
>
>**Column Five** – describe your observable behavior. What did you actually do in response to what you saw, read, or heard?
>
>**Column Six** – rate how you felt on a scale of 1-10. Zero (0) indicates no emotion, while 10 indicates the highest level of emotion. *Do not attach any particular meaning to the rating.
>
>**Column Seven** – record the completion date of your 500 word description of the Gallery moment.

Writing Gallery Log™ 2007

#1 External or Internal	#2 What prompted this specific Gallery Moment	#3 Physical Reaction (tears, smiles, chills,	#4 Thoughts, Feelings	#5 Behavior: Oberservable Reactions (e.g. began writing, silence etc.)	#6 Gallery Rating	#7 Date of 500 word write completed

A Word about Journaling

Journaling provides an opportunity for you to release feelings and emotions about a particular topic or situation, without the burden of perfecting a task. Journaling does not require lengthy preparation or formal training. However, it does require you to make a commitment and spend "quiet time" for "self"—away from others. The process of journaling includes reflection and clearing the mental clutter that inhibits creativity when writing in a more formal setting. Journaling your feelings and current experiences during those writer's block moments can do one of several things:

- Relieve emotional stress
- Encourage better sleep patterns
- Enable you to see areas that need improving or problems to be addressed
- Give you an outlet to freely express concerns, challenges, and fears
- Provide a method of developing future writing topics and goals

Remember, you are investing in yourself. It is important to dedicate time (at least one hour) each day to write about experiences, feelings, issues, and challenges that may affect your writing career. Make sure everyone in your household understands and respects the time you've selected. You may want to begin your journaling time by listening to music and nature sounds, or by reading inspirational verses that encourage mental calm and relaxation. The key is to allow your mind to wander and release thoughts. Since writing is a mental activity, sound machines that provide sounds like water, rain, sounds of the ocean, or birds can be great encouragement to your mental state and general well-being.

Be deliberate in your selection of where you will begin the journaling process. Make sure you are away from noise and chatter, television, radio, and the PHONE! Most importantly, do not apologize for using time for yourself. Just as you schedule time to eat, socialize, attend school, or go to work, schedule time to journal.

Date your journal. Putting a date on your thoughts allows you to note changes and track positive outcomes from your pattern and attitude adjustments. Finally, maintain a positive attitude. Suffering the challenge of writer's block is momentary. Joy does come in the morning, and morning is not a time of day, but rather a state of mind. Write until your joy comes!

Use the sample journal page to begin the journaling process. It is another great strategy for completing your work.

JOURNALING YOUR THOUGHTS

Date: _____   Event: _____

Time: _____   Place: _____

_____
_____
_____
_____
_____
_____
_____
_____
_____
_____
_____
_____
_____
_____
_____
_____
_____
_____
_____
_____
_____
_____
_____
_____
_____
_____
_____

©VMAssociates Writers in the Marketplace, P.O. Box 47182, Windsor Mill, MD 21244
www.theresawilsonbooks.org

Writing Project Development Form

Once you have completed your Gallery writing strategy, the next steps include developing a plan of action leading to completed works. Use the following form to outline topics and ideas that help set the stage for expanded writing and completed projects. You may want to print copies of this form, as it will be necessary to provide an outline for each topic.

PROJECT FOCUS:

( ) Poetry   ( ) Non Fiction Historical   ( ) Non Fiction Research   ( ) Romance
( ) Romantic Mystery   ( ) Inspirational   ( ) How To Non Fiction   ( ) Script
( ) Screenplay   ( ) Other (be specific) _____

PRIORITY:
( ) High   ( ) Medium   ( ) Low

Start Date: _____   **Projected Completion Date:** _____

Specific Challenges/Opportunities to Address: *(e.g. travel time, availability of people and resources, etc.)*

_____
_____

Description/Details: This is where you write the vision or idea for the book, article, poetry, screenplay, etc. Who is the audience? What is the setting? Why did you choose this project?

_____
_____
_____
_____
_____
_____
_____
_____
_____

Don't wish for it. Work for it.

CHAPTER 7

WRITING CRITIQUE GROUPS

THE QUEST FOR APPROVAL

The Quest for Approval

All of us seek positive feedback about our writing. Selected carefully, critique groups can provide a positive, safe environment for sharing thoughts and gaining greater insight about your topics and ideas. There are important considerations to bear in mind as you begin the process of sharing your writing for others to comment and review. Paramount to any review process is your ability to "Manage Your Expectations". It is your responsibility to set the tone for what you hope to gain from sharing your work with others. You cannot assume they know what you want from mere interaction. You must provide clarity and direction.

To ensure the level of "target focused" feedback you require, there are several steps to follow:

1. Know the response you seek: Are you looking for someone to edit your work (e.g. language usage, spelling, sentence structure, etc.), or do you simply want confirmation that your topic is interesting, holds the listener's attention, or has a market?

2. Set the tone for your requests: Be specific about the level of input you desire

- Develop questions around your topic and method of presenting your information. (If content focused, be clear as to whether you want responses about the development of your topic or method.) Can the group follow the main theme? Are the characters' roles clearly-defined, etc.?
- If you have grammar, proofreading, and other formatting related issues, it may be more appropriate to send an advanced copy of your work to the Critique Committee to establish a more specialized forum.
- If you seek ideas for marketing and promotion for your completed work, then a publisher would suit you best. Again, it is important to be specific, as it gives a clearer understanding to

your supporters, who'll in turn offer concrete suggestions and referrals.

3. Develop a Personal Feedback Resource Directory: Gather a list of people who could provide an array of editing, publishing, and marketing related resources and guidance. This may require *"stepping out of the box"* by attending conferences, one-day workshops, or writing classes, all of which help to provide a creative support network of resources. The choice is up to you.

4. Think Outside the Box, so you can connect the *"writing success"* dots. In the illustration below (The Nine Dots, The Complete Games Trainers Play, Edward Scannell and John W. Newstrom, McGraw Hill Publishing, 1994), participants were asked to connect the dots using only four (4) straight lines. The purpose was to demonstrate challenges faced when limiting your ability to think beyond what you perceive.

CAN YOU CONNECT THE DOTS USING 4 STRAIGHT LINES?

0   0   0

0   0   0

0   0   0

Achieving Successful Connection: Only when participants extended their lines outside the parameters of the dots did they realize success "connecting the dots" was a guarantee. We must do the same. When seeking "critique group" support, we must move beyond friends and associates to validate our work, and instead move toward the critique of professional writers whose feedback can potentially launch us to the next level.

A word about family

As a rule, share your writing with family and friends when it is ready. Do not use them as a mechanism to affirm if you're on the right track. Because of their close ties and interest in your success and happiness, they may not always give you the honesty you'll need. Seeking support, encouragement, and feedback for your writing is an art you develop through practice. The process begins with setting the tone.

Remember, only you can define your need. Only you can give clarity about what you hope to gain from the feedback you seek. Without clearly articulating this need, critique group listeners and readers will respond based on their interpretation of the situation—often leaving you unfulfilled and in want.

SAMPLE FOR "CRITIQUE" GROUP COMMENTS FORM

Author's Name _____ Review Date: _____

1. Did the material hold your interest? ( ) Yes, ( ) Somewhat ( ) No If so, why?_____
_____
_____

If not, what do you feel would make the topic more interesting? _____
_____
_____
_____

2. What would a reader gain from the information provided? What's in it for them?
_____
_____
_____

3. Does the author appear knowledgeable about the subject matter at hand, if any? ( ) Yes ( ) No

4. Are the author's thoughts fluid? Is the author sequentially and fully developing their thoughts? ( ) Yes ( ) No
_____
_____
_____

5. Who do you think would be interested in reading this work? Why?
_____
_____
_____

6. Does the writing do one or more of the following:
   - ☐ Does it create an emotion? (pity, happiness, sadness, hopefulness, etc.)
   - ☐ Does it provide inspiration? (encouraging, supportive, creates a need to know more)
   - ☐ Does the writing provoke a "call to action"? (change something, move forward, accomplish a task, etc.)

8. How was Scripture used?
   - [ ] Too much (overused)
   - [ ] Not enough (found areas where quotations are needed)
   - [ ] Balanced (a good combination)

9. Is the author focused (maintains his/her idea)? ( ) Yes ( ) No If no, what suggestions would you offer for improvement: _____
_____
_____
_____

10. Did the writing hold your interest? ( ) Yes ( ) No
_____
_____
_____

CHAPTER 8

HOW TO SUBMIT WORK FOR PUBLICATION

We spend a great deal of time perfecting our literary works, hoping the publisher will take interest. Make no mistake, publishers want to receive good work. Our job is to make sure we submit work that has been carefully prepared, developed and reviewed, so it rises above others' works in the publishing world.

It is recommended that new writers begin by establishing themselves through magazines, devotionals, poetry contributors, and short stories. Doing these work "small" writing works inadvertently begins to establish an audience base that'll stick around for bigger projects, if they like what they see. There are several, basic tips for submitting articles to publishers. They may sound simple, but it is amazing how many of us "misstep" and find our materials rejected. There are no guarantees that, by following these tips, you'll be published. Our goal, however, is to impact the publishing editor in a positive way.

- If submitting work via "mail", make sure it is a visibly clean, typed document.
- Read the publication's guidelines to which you are submitting your work. Make sure your topic is one they cover. If you have a new idea, contact them (via email or mail) and present the idea. Send a query, asking the editor/publisher if they would consider a "unique" approach you've developed for a particular topic.
- Read and FOLLOW the publisher's guidelines for submission. If they do not specify, the normal format includes typing your name and address on the top of each page, providing a word count for the article (again, at the top of the page), and listing an email address. Most publishers require their submissions, and give their responses, via email.
- Be prepared to work with editors. Don't assume your article is ready to print. Often editors will

- like your writing style, but they may need you to add (or delete items) to fit their editing process. If they contact you, focus on being cooperative. Work with them on any revisions needed, so they will wantto work with you again. Establish a reputation of being positive, not stubborn and opinionated. Take the high road in your responses to editors.
- Meet the publisher's deadline. If you have agreed to make required changes, and have been given a deadline, do it! The publishing world is small, and bad news travels fast.

A Word about Contributing Author Agreements:

As you begin to expand and develop your writing, you may consider opportunities to publish via the internet. Sometimes ezine publishers/on-line magazine publishers will require you sign a "contributing author" agreement. It is important to review the details of any agreement to clarify what's expected, what's prohibited, and your rights during publication. For your comfort and protection, before agreeing to any author agreements, keep one or two items in mind:

Terms and conditions should be clear and include details that you, the author, clearly understand. Submission should remain in "author owned" status.

Author fees should be clear. If submissions are non-paid, be sure to submit a by-line (2-3 lines about the author) at the end of your article. By-lines can include author's contact email(s) and web site address(es).

The primary focus of an author-agreement is to protect the ezine publisher from copyright infringement issues because of errors or omissions of others. It also helps in clarifying limitations of contributors. Ezine publishers may revise the terms of an agreement at any time. For your protection, it is always good to review general rules of submission each time you submit and ask questions, if unsure.

The following page provides an example of an author agreement.

Sample Author CONTENT AGREEMENT

The following Agreement is made between _____ (hereinafter known as "Author") and Writers on the Move Magazine, Inc. (hereinafter known as "Publisher"). The Author hereby grants the Publisher the right to publish literary work(s) presented to Publisher by Author (hereinafter called "Work" or "Works") in Publisher owned or managed publications which include but are not limited to, Writers on the Move Magazine and writersinthemarketplace.org's website. In addition, Publisher is granted the absolute right to print and reprint the Work in any publication (electronic, print or otherwise) affiliated with Writers on the Move Magazine, provided full credit is given to the Author. Therefore, the Author consents to and acknowledges the Publisher's right to print and reprint the Author's Work under this Agreement.

The Author maintains the copyright to the Work, and is entitled to submit the Work for publication or to sell the rights to the Work as he/she chooses. This Agreement is valid for all Works previously presented to the Publisher by the Author, as well as present or future Works presented to Publisher by Author.

The Author warrants that he or she is the sole owner of the work and has full power and authority to copyright it and to enter into the Agreement; that the Work does not infringe any copyright, violate any property rights, or contain any scandalous, libelous or unlawful matter. The Author will, to the extent authorized under the laws and constitution of the State of _____, defend, indemnify and hold harmless the Publisher and/or its licensees against all claims, suits, costs, damages and expenses that the Publisher and/or its licensees may sustain because of any scandalous, libelous or unlawful matter contained or alleged to be contained in the Work, or any infringement or violation by the Work of any copyright or property right.

Writers In The Marketplace Press.

By: _____
Title: _____
Date: _____

Author

By: _____
Title: _____
Date: _____
E-Mail: _____

Writing a Query Letter

Often a publisher requires a query (summary of an idea you would like to write) before agreeing to review your magazine article or book proposal. There are several key points to consider when preparing a query letter:

Presentation, Presentation, PRESENTATION! - You have about 10 seconds or 2-3 lines to capture interest or "pitch" your idea. Within that timeframe, you should be able to describe what you're offering, why it's relevant to the magazine or book publisher, and its benefits.

Tips to make it Happen

- Learn as much about the publishing company as possible
- Read their writer guidelines and use their words to describe your topic. If they want children's stories with a holiday theme, start your query with an emphasis on this theme and show the connection with what you are presenting.
- Keep your enthusiasm! Be full of energy and convey belief in how your work (proposal or theme) compliments their overall theme.
- Address the competition – Through your pitch, convey your awareness of the "competition" and their similar work. List one to two sentences that distinguish what you offer.
- Credibility – Be prepared to provide your qualifications to write about your topic of choice. Also, highlight any other literary works, years of expertise, etc.).

WORD OF CAUTION – If you are submitting a query for a proposed book, make sure you have a book proposal and/or completed manuscript ready to submit if requested. You don't want to disappoint an acquisitions editor by stating that you'll need 2-3 months to complete the work. When you query, be ready to submit.

Keep Track of Your Submissions

You'll have the advantage of submitting to multiple publishers at the same time (simultaneous submissions). It's important to keep track of what, when, and where you send your written works. Even magazine articles should be tracked on a regular basis. The following "Writing Submissions Tracking Form" is a sample tool used for keeping track of publishers and submissions.

Submission Tracking Form

Date Sent	Publisher's Name	E-Mail	BP	Article	Query	F / NF / Poetry	Accepted/Rejected	Follow Up Yes / No

Reference Codes: NF = Non-Fiction, F = Fiction, BP = Book Proposal

HOW TO SUBMIT YOUR WORK ON THE WEB

What are Ezine Publications?

An Ezine is nothing more than an electronic newsletter or magazine. Unlike printed magazines, Ezines are usually free and there are thousands of them, under any topic you could possibly consider.

Subscribing to an ezine is like joining a club of people with the same interests. As mentioned above, Ezines are written under almost any topic, such as culinary arts, home and garden, interior design and spiritual/inspirational, to name a few. For your information, provided in the directory of this manual is a link to a list of Ezine directories. Take time to visit and select one of several directories to explore. Whether your interest is writing articles for Ezine, or developing an ezine of your own, knowing of accessible and available options is important.

Ezines thrive on quality content and credibility of its authors. People subscribe to an ezine because they have a need for advice and information or seek comprehensive research on a specific topic. As the editor, you are responsible to ensure this happens, which means you must know the subject, in order to scrutinize the articles you receive. One way to guarantee success is to take the time to write several articles.

"Learning by doing" is the key to success in any endeavor. If you want to publish an ezine, you should understand the "nuts and bolts" of its creation and development. This mainly occurs by personally performing the tasks and functions necessary. Remember, your name and reputation precedes you on this very public communication.

Why use Ezines?

An Ezine can be used as a marketing tool that drives traffic to your web site. It's the "draw" to what you want your visitors to really see. Your web site is the selling point of the product or service, and Ezines can be effective tools for leading potential customers to that site. By writing for an ezine:

- You'll potentially grow more established in an area of expertise. If you're consistent in providing quality content, name recognition is the resulting benefit. Because of your consistency in presenting comprehensive, concise details and descriptions, people will stop to review any new released information from you.
- You're allowed to publicize and promote other articles, books, or previously shared opinions on which you share similar topics.
- You may attach by-lines on the articles. (A by-line is a brief background of the writer's qualifications and can include email and other contact information).
- You are able to provide a direct line to your web site or contact information, thereby increasing
- access and exposure.

SAMPLE EZINE SUBMISSION

Submitting to Ezine Articles.com

STEP #1: Go to ezinearticles.com. Click "Start Your Free Membership"

Note: Take time to review the topics offered. Remember, you can write a book review or write on a topic of interest to others.

STEP #2: You will need to provide contact information (email, password, name, etc.).

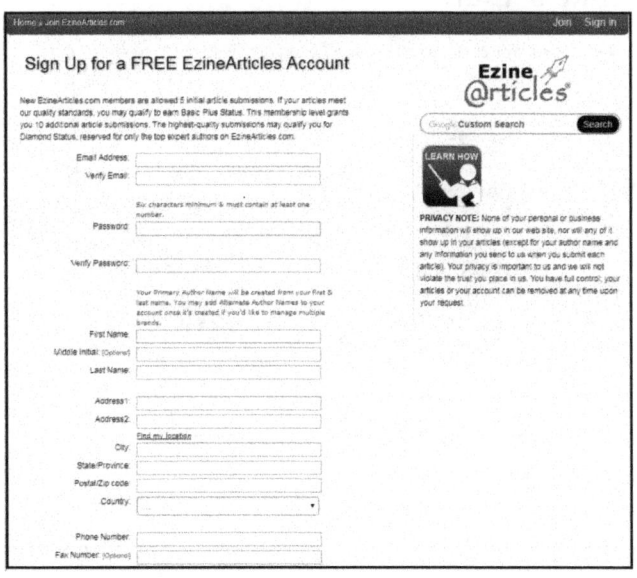

Step #3: Check boxes of preference, answer details to prove you are not a Robot, then click to create an account.

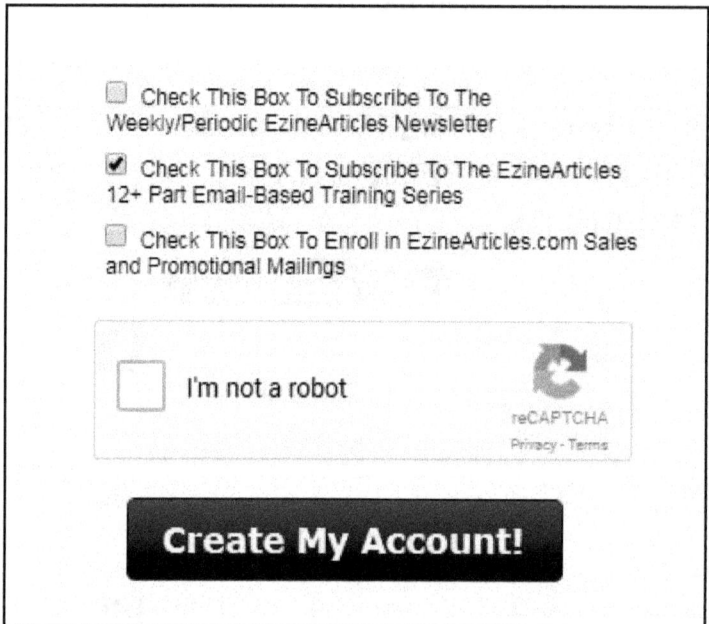

Step #4: Take time to explore Networking Opportunities or you can click to begin to upload an article.

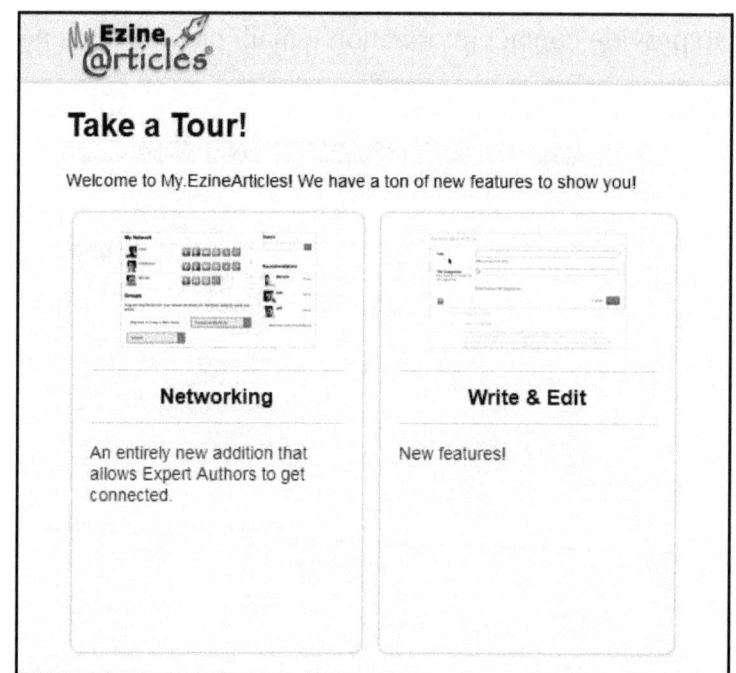

Step #5: If you Click "Networking" you can view information of make a connection with other EZine Authors, join a discussion group, learn how to earn badges, or click "Activity" to learn about what others are doing and how to become a part of the groups.

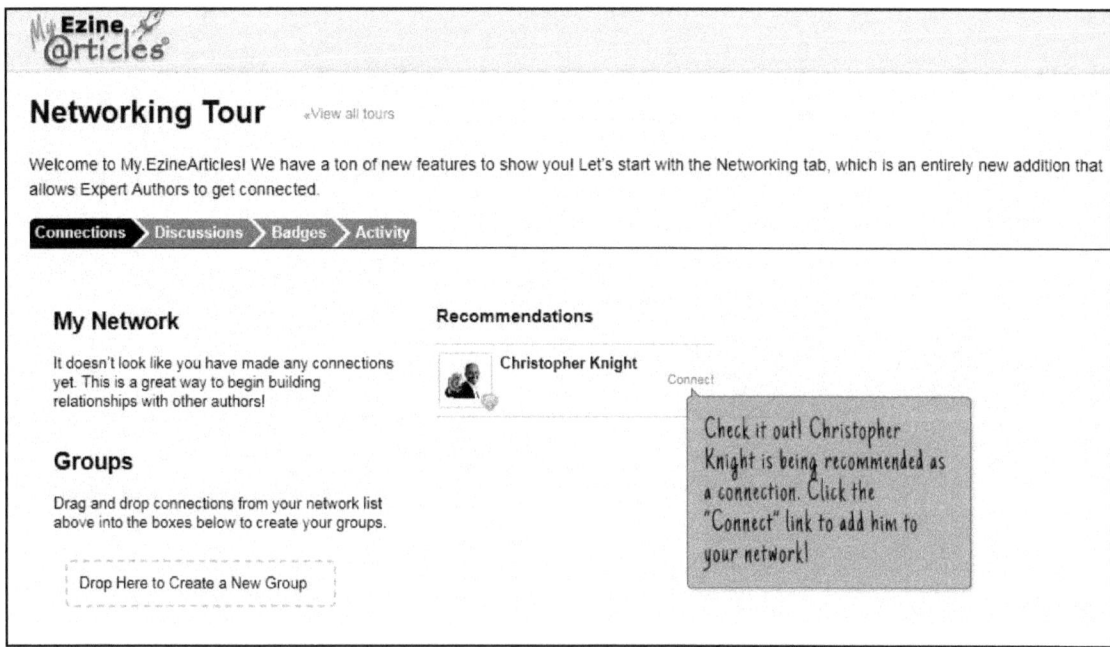

Step #6: If you click "Write & Edit" Tour – You can elect to create a new article, review published and unpublished articles, create and edit your resource box, or search for title suggestions.

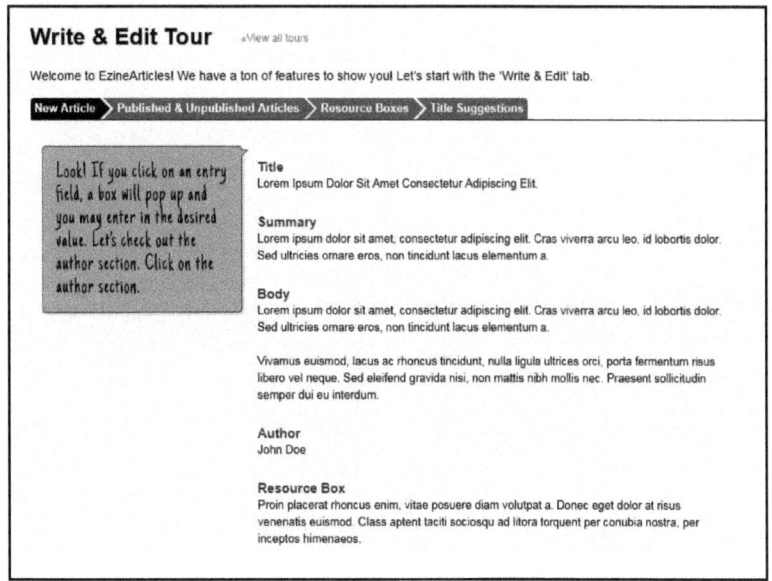

CONGRATULATIONS!! YOU'VE COMPLETED SUBMITTING ONLINE!

CHAPTER 9

BETTER IS ONE DAY:
TAKING ADVANTAGE OF CONFERENCES

The decisions you make about time-management will directly affect whether or not you fulfill your writing assignments. When it comes to improving skills, meeting people of influence, and receiving strategies and tips that potentially grows you into an accomplished writer, I wonder why anyone wouldn't take advantage of attending writers' conferences.

Often, people fall into the "all or nothing" trap believing there isn't much of a benefit to attending writers' conferences. Planned appropriately, attending any one day of a conference will be better than "1,000 elsewhere". While preparing to visit relatives, I learned a writers' conference was scheduled in the next town. Though I was scheduled to assist in a special event (the birth of my grandson), I noticed that at least one day of the two-day schedule included an opportunity to meet with publishers.

Almost immediately, the usual objections began to cloud my thinking. "It can't be done; you don't have the extra funds." "How are you going to fulfill the other obligations?" The conference was during a crucial period, and my presence was expected elsewhere. Being present for my grandson's birth would inhibit my staying an entire day, much less overnight. I made my dilemma known and help was on the way. The answer to this first hurdle came by way of my husband who offered to assist with family assignments, so that I could attend the conference for one day.

With that obstacle resolved, I realized my next challenge was registration costs. I had already expensed budgeted travel monies and really did not have the extra funds needed. I hesitated over this predicament. The challenge was short lived. The organization sponsoring the conference offered small scholarships to defray registration costs.

Before I "chucked" the idea of attending, I prayed, and then wrote to the director of the American Christian Writers Association (ACW) to determine whether there were any scholarships or other resources available. He responded by forwarding the Murphey Foundation Scholarship application. I applied and, to my delight, the registration expenses were covered. Another objection, the finances, was resolved because I listen to and followed what I felt in my spirit. I pressed toward the prize.

I attended the conference, and in that one day, I was able to review updated writer resources and materials, meet and connect with fellow writers, talk with a publishing representative, and submit my book proposal. I left loaded with materials and encouraged to keep writing. It was one of the best single days I've spent in a long time.

Conference Readiness

The time to prepare for attending a writer's conference is NOW. "Be ye ever ready." Waiting only creates pressure and anxiety, should an opportunity become available on short notice.

I benefited by attending the conference for one day, because I prepared with business cards, writing-samples, and book proposals in advance. In addition to having copies of your manuscript and book proposal available, there are several key points to remember when preparing to attend a conference:

Pre-Planning:

- First, **read the details of the conference itinerary** carefully, so that you can plot your course based on timelines and topics. With only a one-day allotment, you do not want to waste time at the event deciding which workshops to review. If possible, have topics and times detailed, so you flow from session to session.
- *Review the listing of faculty, presenters, agents, editor and/or publishers who will attend.* Use the website (www.google.com) to investigate details about those persons of interest. It is advantageous to find photos that permit you to identify them in the crowd and allow for informal introductions long before the 15-minute editor/publisher schedules.
- *Prepare clippings* of any materials you've published, preparing to leave samples of your writing with interested publishers/agents. With only 15 minutes to make a positive impact, it is a great idea to leave the publisher/editor with something by which to remember you. You can also digitally scan the cover of several published magazines that hold your articles or books in which you were a contributing author and distribute them as handouts to the publishers in attendance.
- *Have you completed a manuscript?* Take the time to prepare a "One Page" description of yourproject. This will make a great handout to entice editors to request your book proposal. This one page will include a paragraph about the book, a paragraph about your audience, competitive titles, your marketing plan, and a paragraph about the author. This is a **WOW** letter that"depending upon how much effort you're willing to invest, you could also prepare

the latest marketing tool known as DocuMagnet (distributed by Xerox corporation www.Xerox.com). With DocuMagnet, you can hand the publisher/editor a flyer announcement that includes a magnet with the same information. It is a novel idea that will keep your name in the forefront of their minds. It is important to be creative in developing your "promotional" ideas. Remember, your goal is stand above the crowd. Depending upon the conference size, you may feel more than one sample of your writing is needed. Another appealing tool for marketing your writing is a portfolio. Editors and publishers often attend writers' conferences as presenters and panel members as well as participate in forums to review and critique written work. You, the writing artist, are in the spotlight and must be prepared to "show your best stuff" at a moment's notice. With competition as fierce as it is, the "window of opportunity" to capture an editor's or publisher's attention is narrow unless you pre-plan an appealing marketing tool to distinguish you from the crowd.

The Writer's Portfolio

A writer's portfolio can be a key asset when seeking to impress publishers with the quality of your work. A writer's portfolio should be compact and easy to transport. Each page should include brief and attractive writing samples of your quality work.

Preparation Materials Needed:
- *Loose Leaf Notebook* (Nothing larger than a 1in. binder for easy packing and carrying)
- *Clear Slip Sheets* (These can be purchased at a local office supply store. They are great for protecting individual pages).
- *Scissors* (It is important to trim any magazine or journal clippings to ensure a neat and presentable finish, worthy of adding to your portfolio.

Give your writing portfolio a polished look by using "slip sheets", showing organized division of your work, and to protect the constant handling of hard copies. Consider using a loose-leaf notebook binder, which allows you to move and replace materials easily.

Portfolio content should begin with an attractive cover that includes your name, contact number and a 5-8 lined by-line (brief description of what you have published and/or expertise on topic you propose to write). Your writer's resume (a listing of completed freelance and other writing jobs and assignments) should follow the by-line of your portfolio. It should include a brief overview of your background and experiences as a freelance writer or author, as well as any job-related writing. You might also include a separate slip-sheet for storage of business cards to make them easily accessible and ready for distribution.

The portfolio is helpful in several ways:

- It serves as a single source of your most important writing samples.
- It provides a way to introduce yourself and your work to editors at writers' conferences and seminars.
- It gives quick access to information.
- It demonstrates that you are a serious writer.
- It serves as a great tool for publicizing your writing.

Your writer's portfolio should be handled like a child who is growing, developing, and maturing under your guidance. It will evolve as your writing matures. It is always in transition while exhibiting higher heights and deeper depths of quality content.

- ◊ **Carefully plan your professional look.** "Dressing for success" is a key phrase to remember when attending a writers' conference. If you are serious about promoting your work, always dress like you're ready for a book signing event at any moment. In this day of "too casual", the neat, polished look is still very appealing to editors and publishers. You are representing your work. Un-kept, carefree attire may send the wrong message. While you don't have to dress in a business suit, business casual (always with a jacket handy) will never go out of style. In the end, a person's outward appearance is usually directly correlated to the professionalism level of their writing.
- ◊ **Bring business cards.** Never attend a conference without them. There are website sources like www.vistaprint.com that will enable you to purchase cards inexpensively. Again, it is about the "look" you are catering for business.
- ◊ **Plan to Arrive Early** – The "early bird" really does catch the choice opportunities. Because you may have only one day, it is important to arrive early to select sign-up times conducive to your networking with as many people as possible. Remember, you've investigated and know the people who you mostly want to see. With only one day, there is nothing more disappointing than arriving late and finding your choice is booked.
- ◊ **Move around (work the crowd**)- Introduce yourself to as many fellow writers as possible. Expand your base of associations. Writers need writers for encouragement and support. Determine to achieve a goal of connecting and exchanging business cards with at least three to five new people. No matter your personality style, press to accomplish this task on a regular basis. You never know what one connection will mean for you and for them. "Iron sharpens iron." For writers, it is better to have at least one day of quality time at a conference that connects you to experts, supporters, and peers. The next time the announcement arrives, eliminate the objections, stay in the press, and master every opportunity while there for that one day.

Quick Reminders

- A portfolio is a marketing tool for presenting writing samples (clips) to editors
- A writing portfolio is a vehicle for presenting one's written work
- A portfolio can be as simple as a loose-leaf notebook, with clear, plastic insert covers
- A portfolio will introduce you and your work
- A portfolio makes it easier for editors to assess your writing ability and experience

Pre-Conference Planning Schedule							
				Cost		
Date	Location	Title	Speakers	Travel	Hotel	Food

Final Note: Preparing a Book Proposal for Potential Publishers

Sometimes you will have an opportunity to attend a conference where editors or publishers may ask to review a book proposal (limited to summary and one chapter). Even if they don't read it in yourpresence, be prepared to forward a copy within days of the request. The following is a synopsis of a book proposal's components. Guidelines and format may vary, but all editors and publishers seek a proposal that provides a comprehensive overview of the proposed book project.

Tentative Title: Seldom does your original idea not change towards the project's finale. Be open to suggestions and input from the editor, and lean on their expertise.

Table of Contents: Some publishers require a list of chapter headings. Others will request a 2-3 line summary of each chapter.

What is the Proposed Category for your writing: What is your subject? Where does it fit (e.g. Education, Historical research, Christian study, etc.)? This is an opportunity to help the editor frame the focus of your message.

What is the Potential Market for your book: Who will be interested in reading your material? Be specific. Include gender (where appropriate), age, cultural, etc.

Describe Similar Books: Here is an area where most new writers fail. It is important to research and discover books similar to yours and write a comparison. What makes your approach to a topic unique, different? Pick at least three authors for this comparison.

Promotional Ideas: How will you help promote your book? What experiences do you have with all forms of media? Do you have any experience as a public speaker? Editors/publishers want to know that you recognize the importance of partnering with them to sell your book.

Manuscript Length: Be specific here. Especially for new writers, provide the exact word count of yourmanuscript. (Note: To find the word count – (1) use your cursor to highlight the material; (2) Click "Tools" (3) Click "Word Count". You'll be shown the number of words and characters in the manuscript.

Completion Date: Project a finish date for the project. Note: New writers need to be 99% complete before submitting a book proposal, and provide a date no longer than 60 days of the book proposal submission.

Sample Chapter: Usually requested to be between 3,000 to 3,500 words (one chapter). Again, this will vary depending on publisher.

I cannot overemphasize the importance of editing your work. Once you review for errors, give it to someone (preferably a professional editor) to review. You want to submit the best possible representation of the author. Oftentimes, this is the first and only document the editor or publisher will see. First impressions are truly lasting.

The following Writing Conference Daily Success Plan is a handy tool for planning how you will spend your time during the conference, as well as assess the results of your efforts after the conference.

Writing Conference Daily SUCCESS Plan©

Conference _____   Date _____

Time	Today's Plan of Action
8:00	
8:30	
9:00	
9:30	
10:00	
10:30	
11:00	
11:30	
12:00	
12:30	
1:00	
1:30	
2:00	
2:30	
3:00	
3:30	
4:00	
4:30	
5:00	
5:30	
6:00	
6:30	
7:00	
7:30	
8:00	
8:30	

ACCOMPLISHMENTS

OUTREACH:
# of In-Persons Approached: ____
Number to follow via Phone/Email Contacts: ____
Personal Note Cards to be Sent: ____

WRITING WORKSHOP SESSIONS ATTENDED:
# of Sessions ____   # Attended ____
#In-Person Contacts: ____   #Bus. Cards Collected: ____

NETWORKING:
When responding to "What do you write," how was the question answered? Did you prepare the 15 second response ( ) Yes ( ) No
Stories Told: ____ Business Cards Passed Out: ____

LUNCH TIME
Sat with strangers: ( ) Yes ( ) No
Initiated Discussion: ( ) Yes ( ) #Cards Collected ____

AFTERNOON WORKSHOP SESSIONS:
Of Business Cards Passed Out: ____
Of Editors/Publishers Met: ____
15 Minute Appointments Set: ____

FOLLOW-UP
#Editor Follow Up: ____   # of thank you notes: ____
Phone Contact: ____   In-Person Contacts: ____
Total Note Cards to be Sent: ____
Total Emails to be Sent: ____
Total Book Proposals to be Sent: ____
Other Follow Up:

_____
_____
_____
_____
_____

CHAPTER 10

FREELANCE WRITERS:
WORKING FROM HOME IS A FAMILY AFFAIR

The level and quality of family input and support are often ignored when working from home. Many freelance writing businesses falter because owners fail to take into account naturally occurring adjustments of working out of the home.

Before embarking on any "at home" businesses, take time to explore the idea with everyone involved. Make a list of advantages and disadvantages together. Especially when children are involved, be sure to include them in this important phase of planning, including:

- ◊ Discussing do's and don'ts when the parent is on "work time".
- ◊ Establishing and clarifying "quality time", so you can diffuse any resentment of changes in living patterns.
- ◊ Developing marketing strategies and projections so that each family member feels included in assignments and business related "jobs".

How Will You Know If You Are Ready?

Home-based businesses are more than a run-of-the-mill idea. One important consideration is ensuring an interest and capability in, and of what you're doing. Ideally, it should be an idea or profession where you great expertise. If you haven't fully developed your idea, take the time to investigate and explore it from various viewpoints.

How Much Money Will You Need?

Establish a budget, so that overhead costs are clear and concise. Decide which luxury items must be sacrificed or delayed during the business start-up phase. What family vacations, if any, will be delayed? How long? Being up front and open with your family in the beginning of your work-at-home planning can help eliminate unnecessary disappointments later. Use the following form to help with that process.

Analyzing Your Expenditures

Monthly Expenses

Monthy Expenses	Cost	Month	Date
Mortgage / Rent			
Groceries (food)			
Home Insurance			
Personal Loans			
Car Payments			
Car Maintenance			
Car Insurance			
Misc Transportation			
Health Insurance			
Other Medical Costs			
Other Insurance			
Electricity			
Heating			
Water & Sewer			
Telephone			
Internet Fees			
Cable TV			
Other			

Do You Have Products (Books) or Idea Worth Selling?

This is where a family's input becomes an immeasurable tool. Your family is your first line of prospecting and sales. You can start by presenting your ideas as part of a family meeting. Your presentation should be thorough and professional, as if you are about to make the most important sale of your career.

Encourage family members to role-play as editors, publishers, or general audience. This strategy helps you to gain from an "in-house" critique of your idea before it goes public. By doing some of these activities, your family's understanding and perspective of your new role will broaden, ultimately urging them to come alongside.

Your level of success in working at home is measured by the amount of input and time you invest in your business. It is improved because of the quality partnerships you develop with people as close as the kitchen-table. If you include your family in the very beginning of the planning process, they will be your foundation of support and encouragement through all stages.

There are several sites you can explore for Freelance writing opportunities:

MediaBistro

https://www.mediabistro.com/jobs/

On this site, you have an opportunity to search for full or part-time freelance writing assignments.

Freelance Writing.com

https://www.freelancewriting.com/

A site that includes access to higher paying writing assignments. Here, you can join writing platforms and enter contests. Open to beginners and established writers.

This Old House

https://www.thisoldhouse.com/tell-us-your-story

This site is interested in articles from people who did their own home renovations. Submit copies of "before and after" photos, a floor plan, and a brief description of your work to: This Old House/ Reader Remodels, 135 W. 50th Street, 10th Floor, New York, NY 10020 Or, email images and information to: readerremodels@thisoldhouse.com You receive a payment of $250 if your home is featured.

Fiverr

https://www.fiverr.com/

Fiverr is a popular freelance marketplace where you can find a variety of writing opportunities from blog posts to press releases to research to legal writing. This is not a high paying site, but gives you much-needed experience. Typically pays $5-$10 per post.

Freelance Writing Jobs

https://allfreelancewriting.com/freelance-writing-jobs/

At this location you can quickly find freelance writing jobs based on dates and pay ranges. Note: This author does not recommend or endorse any of these sites. It is your responsibility to read all requirements before posting your work.

CHAPTER 11

DISPELLING THE MYTH
ABOUT SELF PUBLISHING

Dispelling the Myth about Self-Publishing

When it comes to self-publishing, you are the common denominator for success. The process begins with your commitment to be involved in every step of the process. It will not happen without you accepting that your responsibility for launching the vision, deciding the look, knowing your audience, managing production time, and ensuring a positive outcome. Your first step in the cycle must include understanding the parameters of becoming an Independent Publisher. Because you will incur all expenses related to press and print, a successful outcome will be the result of setting goals and develo ing a detailed budget. Take time to outline anticipated costs involved in self-publishing, as higher fees usually correlate to high quality products. Publishing costs can include:

Editing/Proofreading Costs

◊ Proofreading Cost could be as low as $2/$3.00 per page based on 200-300 words per page. It checks theme fluidity, and for other consistencies and redundancies.

◊ Copyediting is specific to punctuation, grammatical errors, and spelling.

Selecting Book Cover Design

◊ Exploring designs that will convey your book's message should not be taken lightly. Yourchoice of cover color, photos, and designs need to match your themed message to your audience.

◊ Making a book-cover selection should be delayed until you have completed the final copyedits. You will be surprised at the number of times you will choose to revisit the book designlook before making a final decision. Don't rush the process. Taking time to reflect on what you want displayed to the public will save time, money, and regret.

Typesetting
- ◊ Researching and interviewing a professional typesetter to prepare final draft for printing. This relationship is almost as important as the one you develop with your editing consultant. An experienced typesetter takes time to learn the client and will ask questions if they find an area is unclear or appears missing. This is your "baby" and your typesetter is the "god-parent".
- ◊ Reviewing, revising, and rewriting your final copy. This is tedious work, requiring your attention to details. Remember, the final copy represents YOU!

Printing Costs
- Deciding which "Print on Demand" (POD) company to use should be approached carefully -Deciding between paperback or hard-cover for your book's outer shell: "perfect binding" or "saddle stitched"
  Do your research. There are several print distributor options
    - ◊ Lulu
    - ◊ Ingram Spark
    - ◊ Hillcrest
    - ◊ Lightning Source
    - ◊ CreateSpace
    - ◊ Matador
- Explore information provided by the company and assess your potential investment based on your goals
  - ◊ Is this an e-book?
  - ◊ How do you plan to distribute your product (Your website only? Local bookstores?)
  - ◊ What is your budget? This can determine your direction
- Deciding paper quality (paper weight; paper texture; color). Decisions made here affect final costs for production. Some self-publishing services offer a calculator to help determine best direction before printing
- Deciding the number of copies to order during an initial printing (some on-demand publishing companies have minimum order requirements). It is important to know this information before signing a contract

Deciding to Purchase an ISBN# and Bar Code:
ISBN is the acronym for International Standard Book Number. According to www.Bowker.com "the

purpose of the ISBN is to establish and identify one title or edition of a title from one specific publisher and is unique to that edition, allowing for more efficient marketing of products by booksellers, libraries, universities, wholesalers and distributors." It takes 15 days or less, depending upon payment, to get at this number—sold as single number or in amounts of 10 per order. The ISBN identifies the product. Bookstores, libraries and internet retailers will not consider displaying your book without an ISBN, which they use to track the product as part of stock control. Below is a picture-view and identity of the contents of the ISBN.

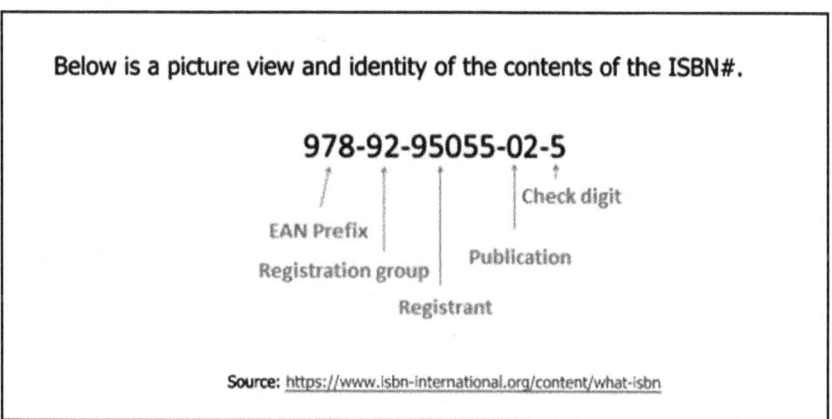

The Process Purchasing the ISBN#

The book publisher applies for the ISBN. If you go the route of self-publishing, you are the Independent Publisher responsible for producing the work. To purchase an ISBN, go to: https://www. isbn.org/ and follow steps below.

Step 1: Click "Buy your ISBNs today"

Step 2: Select the "Buy button" for the number of ISBNs you plan to purchase:

Note: If you are planning a series of books, purchasing 10 ISBNs might be the best selection

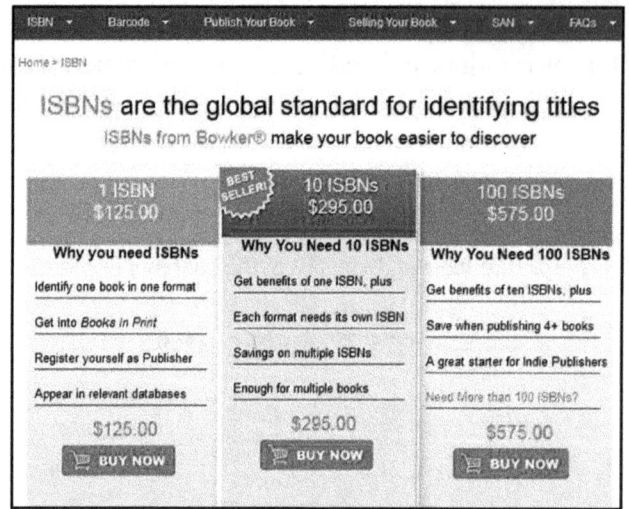

Step 3: Once you click the "Buy Now" button, a page will appear for final purchase.

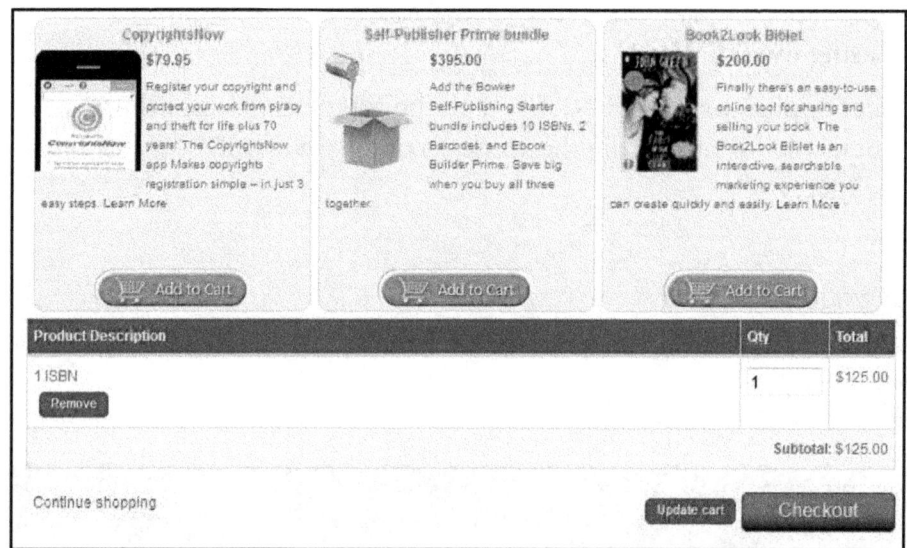

Only after purchasing the ISBN can you purchase a bar code. The following link provides access to this process https://commerce.bowker.com/BarCode. Note: Purchasing a bar code is not mandatory.

Bowker's Bar Code Application

This form should be completed only by those publishers requiring bar codes for existing ISBN Publisher Prefixes. If you are a new publisher needing ISBNs, please to complete the necessary ISBN application form. To order bar codes, you must have ISBNs. The picture below is a sample of the Bowker Code Application page. Just click the "Order Bar Codes" line to begin.

Use Bowker's Bar Code service to:
- Save time and effort in acquiring bar codes with electronic "one stop shopping."
- Receive uniformly accepted bar code files of the highest quality.
- Acquire the new EAN-13 bar codes! The book industry now recommends the ISBN-13 to be displayed above the bar code.
- Learn how and where to use your bar codes.

Click to Order Bar Codes Now!
ISBN 978-0-8352-5555-4

Next, complete application details and pay.

Company/Publisher Name:

Street 1:
Street 2: (optional)
City:
State:
Zip/Postal Code:
Country: United States
Phone #:

ISBN/Bar Code Coordinator: First Name   Last Name

The pricing structure for bar codes is as follows ...

1 - 5 : $25 per bar code
6 - 10 : $23 per bar code
11 - 20 : $21 per bar code

How many bar codes will you be ordering at this time?

Total Bar Codes:
  Total Cost: $ update cost

If you require more than 20 bar codes, please contact us at barcodes@bowker.com.

If you already have ISBNs and wish to register you book(s) titles in Books in Print, you can visit this link and can complete an on-line form to request this registration of your book. Again, http://www.bowkerlink.com/corrections/common/home.asp should only be followed AFTER you have your ISBN and Bar Code.

According to Bowker, "This free portal allows you to market titles through Bowker products to many sectors of the book industry including wholesalers, distributors, retail chains, independent retailers, online retailers, schools, libraries, and universities." Again, you should only register under "Books in Print" after you have your ISBN and Bar Code. Once you purchase an ISBN number, you are considered a publisher. The following forms will be useful as you decide whether or not you should self-publish.

SELF PUBLISHING ASSESSMENT

Level 1

Issue: Deciding whether or not to Self-Publish (Basic Analysis)
Strategies for making decisions: (Write three detailed points specific to each heading)

Budget Analysis "Key Point" Results as of _____ (Date)
- a._____
- b._____
- c._____

Family Input/Support _____ (Date)
- a._____
- b._____
- c._____

Status of Knowledge about Self Publishing Process _____ (Date)
- a._____
- b._____
- c._____

Level 2

Issue: Results of Search for Self Publishing Company
Strategies for making Self-Publishing decisions: (List three main points based on the search of at least three Self-Publishing Companies)

Publisher Name: _____ (Search Date) _____
- a._____
- b._____
- c._____

Publisher Name: _____ (Search Date) _____

a. _____
b. _____
c. _____

Publisher Name: _____ (Search Date) _____

a. _____
b. _____
c. _____

Level 3

Issue: Results of Content Readiness for Self Publishing

Strategies for making Self-Publishing decisions: (List three main aspects of Manuscript and related printed materials)

1. **Status of Manuscript:** ( ) incomplete ( ) in editing (Completion Date) _____

a. _____
b. _____
c. _____

2. **Book Cover:** ( ) In design stage ( ) Needs Designer (Completion Date) _____

(use this space for specific details to be addressed)

a. _____
b. _____
c. _____

3. **ISBN#:** ( ) Yes ( ) No **Bar Code** ( ) Yes ( ) No Date: _____

4. **Endorsement Status** ( ) Yes ( ) No

(use this space to list endorsements or "praise" comments and source)

a. _____
b. _____

A Word about protecting your work: The Copyright Process

According to copyright.gov "Copyright is a form of protection grounded in the U.S. Constitution and granted by law for original works of authorship fixed in a tangible medium or expression. Copyright covers both published and unpublished works. In general, you do not have to register. Copyright exists from the moment the work is created. You do have to register if you wish to bring a lawsuit for infringement of a U.S. work." The process used to copyright your work can be initiated by following the steps outlined below:

1. Go to htttps://www.copyright.gov/
2. Click REGISTER (Register a Copyright)
3. You will land on the Registration Portal page. Click "Log in to the Electronic Copyright Office (eCORegistration System
4. A page will appear for you to create your account, if you have never registered before.

Note: Registrations are for copyrights of completed work. You may also pre-register "if you think it is likely that someone may infringe on your work before it is released, and you have started your work but have not finished it."

According to Copyright.gov, requirements for pre-registration include:

- Your work must be unpublished
- The work must be in the process of being prepared for commercial distribution in either physical or digital format
- The work must be a type of work determined by the Register to have had a history of infringement prior to authorized commercial distribution.

CHAPTER 12

DEVELOPING A SOCIAL MEDIA PRESENCE:

BECOMING YOUR OWN MARKETING EXPERT

Developing the Writer's Web Site: Becoming Your Own Expert

Promoting and marketing your writing is challenging enough without the additional financial burden of hiring a web site expert to put your vision in view. If you are working on a "shoe string" budget and want to make sound money management decisions, avoid hiring a web consultant to make mere, basic adjustments to your site, when it'd be less expensive and just as easy for you to do it yourself.

It is not necessary to be a computer "wiz" to develop your web site. You should know your product and be able to follow directions. Even if you hire a web site consultant, "hands on" content and presentation development will be your responsibility. The buck stops with you. Before you turn over that web site project to an expert, consider the following:

Use web site packages that provide "one-stop-shop" software with built-in features and options, allowing you to build your site using your personal touch. The packages offer 24 hours, 7 days per week control, as opposed to contracting someone $450-$600 for initial development, and then pay $50-$75 per hour to generate the changes in content that'll inevitably come as you grow your business.

Let's look at the basics of web site development for a five-page web site:

What colors do you want your visitors to experience? Choose colors for background and word print. Depending upon the web site service(s) or product(s) you buy, it will be either a soft gray background with black ormaroon print. Others have pastel colors with soft print. Colors are based on the message.

What information should your visitors see first? Your "welcome page" is like the "welcome mat at your door", as it is one of the first things your visitors will see. You are introducing your product (Book, E-Zine, or Newsletter) to the world. Make this page an overview of what your visitors can expect to find on each of the subpages, letting potential customers know they are in the right place.

Who are you? The "About Us" page is your "brag bag" opportunity. It is a place where you talk about your accomplishments and writing experience. This page should be fine-tuned on a regular basis. Wording, pictures, and headings may need revision as you develop and grow your business.

What are you selling? Here is your sales pitch opportunity page. Describe how your product (book, freelance service, etc.) will be useful to your target market. Why is it unique? Why should they purchase it or become regular visitors?

Consultant Decision. If you decide to hire a web site consultant, make sure you have direct contact during all phases of development. Prepare a list of questions, including clarity about your level of control over your site, how they charge for maintenance, and exactly what's included in the basic development package. Be sure the final contract for service is documented in writing, and includes a termination agreement clause, without penalties.

Website Development Checklist

In his article, Blueprint to Develop a Great Website, Michael Ruffini states, "Just like building a house, building a web site requires a blueprint. No one would ever think of building a house without a blueprint, or without knowing what tools to use to build the house." Please use the following list of questions as your guide to planning and developing your web site:

Basic Questions:

1. What is the purpose of your website? Why do you feel you need a website presence?

2. Do you have a name for your site?

3. Do you have a logo?

4. Do I know who my audience will be? (Who will visit your site? Do you know what appeals to your audience?)

5. What is the content for your web site? How detailed will it be? What are your objectives in presenting the content? (What do you hope your visitors will gain from reviewing your materials?)

6. How will you present your topics? How will the site "map" look?

7. Do you know your competitors? Have you visited their sites?

8. How will your web site rank among your competitors?

9. How will you maintain your website? (Who will edit the content and give updates? Are you able to make changes or corrections? How often do you plan to add new content?)

10. How will you measure or determine that your website is a successful investment?

A word about SEO (Search Engine Optimization)

While developing your website, it will be important to keep your goals in mind. You want your site to be attractive and useful. Your focus, therefore, should be threefold:

◊ Connecting to the right systems to keep your web site accessible.
◊ Creating a web "presence" to increase your site's searchability.
◊ Establishing relationships with your visitors to maintain SEO.

According to Wikipedia encyclopedia, search engine optimization (SEO) "is the process of improving the volume and quality of traffic to a web site from search engines. Typically, the earlier a site appears in the search engine results list the more visitors it will receive from the search engines." The content on your web site pages should be written in such a way that it makes your site easier to find, thereby increasing your presence. How? Write content that is interesting, informative, honest, and helpful to your readers. Because search engines love words, the more quality content you write per page, the better.

Other important tools include:
◊ **Title Tags** –should include key words and phrases, and a comprehensive description of what-the page is about. According to SEO Logic (www.seologic.com), Title Tags are used by web-masters and other when the link to your web page. A well-written site is reviewed quickly. Title Tags are displayed in search results and are used by major search engines.
◊ **Meta Tags** –these are target keywords and phrases that search engines pick up. They are the-foundation of the search engine optimization process. If you do nothing else, explore thesetwo areas, so that your efforts to develop your web site reap positive results. Your first and mostim-portant goal is to be found by as many people as possible.

Promoting Your Web Site: Using Social Networking Sites

Social Networking sites have become a great resource for anyone interested in getting free exposure for their products or services. Once you've published, social networking will help establish a following-for your work and maintain relationships for future endeavors.

The purpose of Social Networking is to bring people together with similar interests, creating a relaxed atmosphere for sharing and exchanging ideas. Social Networking can also help people share interests with people around the world. The biggest draw to this medium of communication is that it's accomplished in places of your choosing. Social Networking helps build lasting relationships, expose you to others as an individual and as a writer, and could eventually create sales opportunities for your literary works.

Though there are several hundred social networking sites, Facebook, Twitter, YouTube, and LinkedIn are four you may hear about most often. The following section lists a brief overview of a few of the social media sites.

FACEBOOK
(www.facebook.com)

- ◊ Is a free-access social networking site in which users can join networks organized by city, workplace, school, and region to connect and interact with other people.
- ◊ Facebook was originally created for college students to keep in touch with classmates on campus and to contact their professors.
- ◊ Facebook Sites can include:
  - Your name
  - Your profile-picture
  - Hometown location
  - Political views, interests, activities, books of interest

Copies of photos

"About Me" section (your relationship status, your dating interests, your educational history, network affiliations, etc.)

Take time when deciding what information to place on this site, as with all social media sites. Your photos and comments are permanent and belong to Facebook.

Setting Up a Twitter Account
www.twitter.com

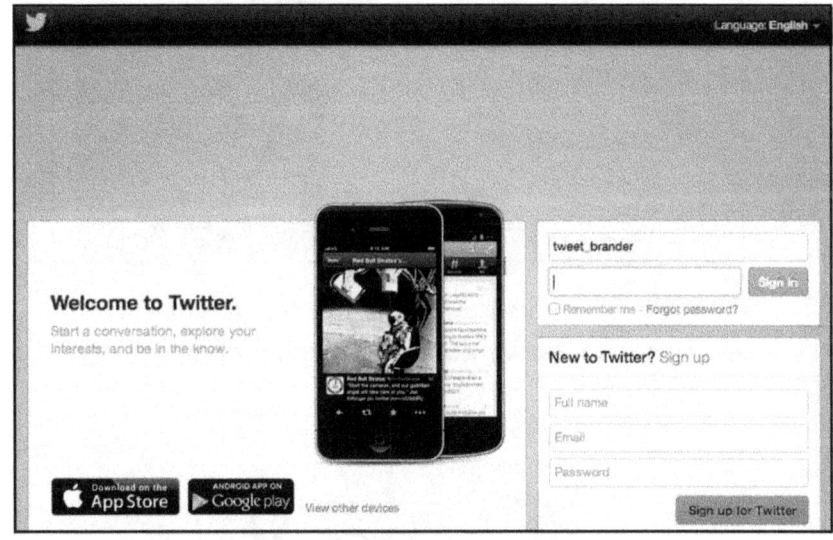

Benefits:
- ◊ Enables users to send and read other users' updates called "Tweets" Tweets are posts of up to 140 characters displayed on the user's profile page and delivered to other users who have subscribed and are known as "followers"
- ◊ Provides free Micro-blogging services
- ◊ Users can send and receive tweets via the Twitter website

Opening Account

1. Enter your Full name, Email address and password to create your Twitter account.

2. Click on "Sign Up" for Twitter and on the next page, Twitter will use your name as username, if it's available.

3. Click on "Create My Account", and "Next Steps". You will receive an Email from the Twitter verification team. Click on the link in the Email to verify your account.

4. Complete your Twitter Profile

Instagram
(www.instagram.com)

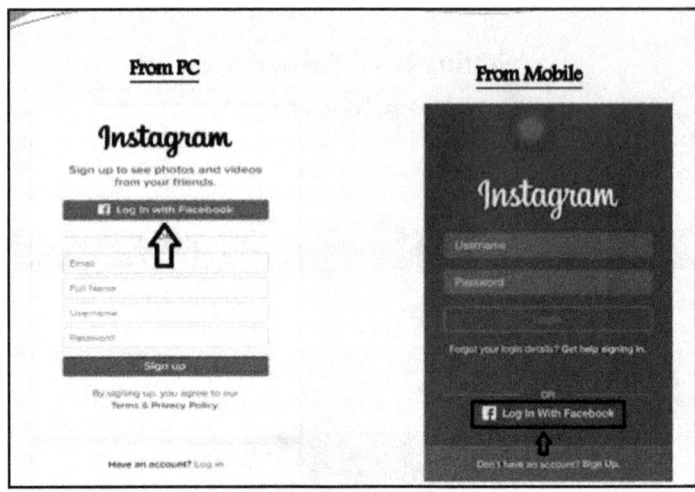

Instagram is a social networking app made for sharing photos and videos from a smartphone. Launching this site is simple. Go to www.instagram.com and complete log-in details.

Setting Up a Pinterest Account

Pinterest is a tool that helps you discover and save creative ideas.

To request an invitation:

1. On the Pinterest home page, click the large, red "Request an Invite" button at the top. A form will appear.

2. Enter your e-mail address and click the "Request Invitation" button. After this, Pinterest will send you an invite. **If you're new to Pinterest, ensure that your profile is complete & optimized before moving forward.**

- Complete Your Profile on Your Biz Account…
- Verify Your Website…
- Set Up Pinterest Rich Pins…
- Learn Pinterest's Terminology…
- Set Up Pinterest Boards…

- Find & Pin Content...

Setting Up a Linked In Account

To join LinkedIn and create your profile:

Go to the LinkedIn sign up page.

- Click the prompt which you're most interested in.
- Type your first and last name, email address, and a password you'll use.
- Click "Join Now".
- Complete any additional steps as prompted.

Setting Up a YouTube Account (You will need a Google Email address)

1. Go to YouTube.com and Click "Sign In".

2. Once you've signed in, you'll see your channels and recommendations of various sites to follow.

CHAPTER 13

EXPANDING YOUR MARKET:
CREATING AN AUDIOBOOK

The decision to create an audio version of your book, though worthwhile, can be a tedious and time consuming undertaking—depending upon the choices you make during the implementation process. It is extremely pivotal and advantageous to hire professional audio producers who'll record your written works in a controlled environment, or sound proof studio, to ensure that quality acoustics and reduce noise interruption. The ultimate goal is to do whatever you can to create a "recording" space, free of outside interference or disruption.

Creating the Audiobook Using a Professional Team

1. The advantage of utilizing a professional recording studio group includes:
2. Knowledgeable and experienced producers
3. Producers who'll oversee the uploading and editing
4. Producers who'll review and monitor recorded material

Producers who'll moderate tone and pitch during the recording process as the author, you are required to:

- Know your material.
- Practice reading aloud, to gain a sense of the flow needed when recording.
- Focus on tone/inflection, so that you read your material with emphasis and proper enunciation at points in your work you wish your audience to remember.
- Listen to your recording with a critical "objective" ear. If you find you can't project the tone or express the feeling you want from your message, be honest with yourself and seek a professional reader for your work.

- Be mindful not to rush to complete your audio recording. This is not an inexpensive project and you want to end with a product worthy of public distribution.

Narrating your audio book has its advantages. For certain, no one knows your work better than you. It's your subject, your story, and is detailed the way you want your message to be conveyed. When you are narrating, you control the pace and have a unique opportunity to express your thoughts to your listeners in the tone and manner that fits the message and meaning of your work. There is nothing more exciting than to give birth to your product at your own pace and tone.

I would be remiss if I did not warn you of the importance of looking carefully before you leap into this project. Weigh all your options carefully. If you decide to pay for professional services, be sure to prepare a service contract that includes, but not limited to:

- The exact number of purchased recording hours.
- The number of sessions included in the contractual cost.

Any other associated services (e.g. creating mp3 files, design of CD cover, cost of finished production). These are details you don't want to be negotiating midway. Once you have clarity about the amount of recording hours included in the contract, monitor that time so that you are not re-negotiating additional recording hours. Publishing is a business—your business! Stay on top of your production related costs and time, so that you do not find yourself financially challenged or in need of extended recording or editing time.

As with writing your book, play, or song, remember this is your product. You have the ultimate say on the look and "feel" of your work. Your pause, pitch, and tone are controlled by you. Those you hire to record/ produce your work may not have the same "buy-in" to the quality of its completion as they would if it were their own product. This is only human nature. Though they may take pride in their work, the level of quality will depend on what you require of them for the completion of tasks. Nothing personal, but this is a business for them. You are ultimately responsible for the quality of the final product.

Audio Recording Tools:

If you decide to create your own audio book, there are several options you can use to make this happen:

1. To use with your Android or iPhone Device, purchase a quality external recording microphone
2. Locate and download the App, "Voice Recorder"
3. Attach the external microphone to your phone
4. Open the Voice Recorder App and press record when ready (Note: You are able to moderate your tone and pitch by watching the "bars" on your phone as they respond to your speech. Be sure to keep the microphone 6 to 8 inches from your mouth when recording)

Once complete, give your recording a title and save it as an mp3 file (Note: You can record and re-record a segment as many times as you feel necessary to ensure an acceptable product.)

Windows Media

According to basic Google guidelines, the following are quick steps to creating an audio file using Windows Media Play:

1. Verify a microphone installation on your Windows PC
2. Click "Start" and type "Sound Recorder" in the search box
3. Click on "Sound Recorder" when you find it in the search box
4. Click "Start Recording," and record your message

In Summary, when it comes to deciding to create an audio book, you should:

1. Remember the importance of being consistent in your use of tone, pitch, and in your pronunciation of words. The "Sound Recorder" is an intelligent system; if your voice or pitch changes too often, it could detract from the quality of the information presented.
2. Avoid extraneous noise at all costs. You'll want your presentation to be viewed as professional, clear, and precise.
3. If you plan to produce your own audio book, take time to review the requirements of the siteon which you intend to upload your files. All sites have specific restrictions on what constitutes acceptable audio file submission. Save yourself time and undue frustration by reading, inadvance, the requirements for submitting your work for production.
4. If you use a professional group to produce your work, be sure to have expectations in writing, leaving no assumptions between both parties.
5. Get it in writing! Before exchanging monies, put into writing any verbal agreements/promises to ensure production expectations are understood and met by both parties

Promoting Your Audio Work

After creating your audio production, be sure to share the news of your project with people as soon as possible. Doing this allows you to expand awareness of your product and encourage conversations about its quality and benefit to others.

Connecting with people via social media allows you to "spread the word" about your work faster than any offline communication method. In addition to Email, there are several social media sites you can use to promote your work:

- Facebook
- Twitter
- YouTube
- LinkedIn

- Instagram

Of course, you can also still use "Email."
- ◊ Send your contact persons a published sample of your audio book.
- ◊ Send your contact persons periodical brief updates
- ◊ Always share anything new or noteworthy about you and your work
- ◊ Invite your contact persons to any book signings or author events
- ◊ Make use of every opportunity to expand your contact persons list

Audio CD Available at www.theresawilsonbooks.com

CHAPTER 14

CREATING "YOUR" WRITERS
VISION BOARD

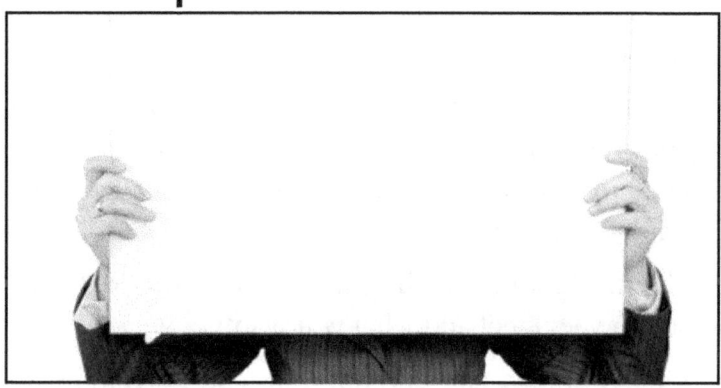

If you have spent any amount of time on Facebook, Twitter, Instagram, or Pinterest, chances are you've seen or heard Vision Boards mentioned at some point. It's a concept that's discussed in board rooms, sales meetings, and even in classrooms. Vision boards are popular because they're great tools for getting you from the dream/vision phase to actually completing the set goal.

It's typically described as a special place to post visuals of ideas and concepts you want to see come to life. It's an incubator for the dream—a place where you can attach pictures to model future steps toward something you have imagined or dreamed.

Do you have a dream of a national magazine featuring your literary work? To start your vision board, you could:

- Attach the magazine cover of the magazine you wish to be featured in, on poster board.
- Create a photo of yourself on this magazine cover. (This is very easy to do with Apps like "Photo in Hole"). Print the copy and post on the board.
- Surround your picture with action words and/or phrases that provoke you towards your goal. Examples of phrases: "Goals for Completion", "Submission Date", "Word Count", "Clear Topic", "Successful Completion", "Reached the Goal", "Money", and "Recognition".

Your vision board may also be developed based upon your desired outcome for your published book. Here are a few tips for this method:

- Surround your book cover with the book covers of your favorite authors.
- Create mock endorsements that you'd love to receive from these authors about your book.
- Take pictures of the authors and place them beside your own photos as a vision of your meet-

ing these authors one day.
- Cut printed images and phrases awards ceremonies that relate to your passion, such as the Grammys.
- Add pictures of Annual Book Award emblems to your board for inspiration.
- Add to this board "ACTION Words" or phrases that provoke you to move forward to achieve the goal.

Other Vision Board Preparation Tips to Consider:
1. Your Vision Board can and should include testimonials or comments about your previous work(s). Seeing these comments on a regular basis often creates the boost we need to keep pressing toward completion. Writers can be their own worst enemies. Because of our critical nature, we can talk ourselves into self-doubt and out of success better than anyone.
2. Don't get bogged down in structure; there are no rules. This is YOUR vision board! Do YOU and make it about how you feel and what you want.
3. Use "Post Its" or hand-printed tape-slip notes instead of typing your goals and objectives. There is something about seeing your own handwriting that keeps your Writer's Vision Board personal to you.
4. Don't limit yourself to one board. You can create a vision board within a vision board for one of your book chapters—the chapter that is giving you the most challenges. Create a board about the characters: Define their personality? How do you want them to appear to the reader? What is the destiny for this character? How does he/she look in your mind? Find and attach pictures that best describe the way you see your characters.

Before You Begin: Basic Vision Board Supplies
Here is a checklist of items to have on hand **before** initiating your Vision Board process:
- Gather magazines, newspapers, vacation destination photos, old portfolios, any books you've written, or any images that spark your creative juices.
- Include all the items you review regularly when writing (notebooks, journals, calendar reminders, testimonials, text messages or emails from friends, and/or postcards) that remind you of places you've visited.
- Start with a blank board. (poster boards, easel charts, and cork boards are great inexpensive purchases)
- Make sure to have easy access to scissors, tape, push pins, and glue sticks. This may sound elementary, but realizing you're missing the most basic of necessities can be an excuse used to put off this exercise to another day, which never comes. Don't sabotage what can be a very worthwhile exercise because you weren't prepared to begin. Be mindful of "self-inflicted" failure.

Before You Begin: Set the Atmospheric Tone for Creating Your Vision Board

The environment, your "emotional thermometer", and your mood are very important for setting the tone for your Writer's Vision Board process. It's absolutely necessary to remove any distractions, including cell phones, access to social media sites, and radio and T.V. background noise. This atmospheric "cleansing" also includes friends and family "getting the boot". It may only be for an hour or so, but this is hour is precious. You can always host a 'Vision Party' with friends, but the Writer's Vision Board is very specific to your tasks as an author and is best created with little or no distraction until completion. After these steps, sharing your board and exchanging board ideas with other writers could be very fun and useful.

Once you've completed your board, hang it in a prominent location to see it regularly. This is what makes it a VISION BOARD. Your board is "fluid" in nature, which means you are adding, removing, and rearranging items on this board regularly. As your writing goals change, the vision for achieving those goals will most likely change, as well.

Glossary, Writing Conferences, On-Line Writer Resources, and Places to Submit

Glossary of Terms

Autobiography: background, life story.

All Rights: the publication company owns the rights to publish the work worldwide. They do not own the copyright

Advance: money paid by the publisher to the author before the book has been published. The amount is usually based on projected royalties.

Assignment: an article or book the editor or publisher has requested written based on an agreed amount.

Anthology: a collection of short stories written by various authors, compiled in one book or journal.

Bio: usually written in 3rd person, bio is a short description of the writer

Biography: a life story of someone other than the writer

Blank Verse: poetry that doesn't rhyme.

Book Proposal: summary, market plan, 2-3 chapters of the book, overview of competition, and table of contents of proposed book.

Byline: author's name and brief information. Usually 20-50 word maximum, information printed on articles and other published works.

C.B.A.: Christian Booksellers Association. The annual CBA conference is an event where publishers display books for selection by bookstore owners. This event is usually held in July.

Clip: a published article the writer can use as an example of completedwork.

Copyright: belonging to author; no one else can lay claim.

Cover letter: brief introductory letter accompanying a complete manuscript or book proposal.

Edit: to review and mark corrections to written work (grammatical, spelling, errors in facts).

Editor: a publisher's staff member who's responsible for soliciting and reviewing written work for possible publication.

Fiction:	books or stories that are imaginary, not grounded in facts.
Freelance:	work not assigned.
Genre:	kind of writing: fiction, poetry, non-fiction.
Ghost Writer:	you are being paid to write for another. Credit for work is given to another person (no byline).
Guidelines:	publisher's instructions for writing and submitting work.
Kill Fee:	payment given if the magazine cannot or decides not to use the material submitted; usually a negotiated item.
Lead Time:	the time between getting the assignment to write an article and its actual publication; used with seasonal articles and stories.
Manuscript:	book, article, or screenplay.
Novella:	a work of fiction; usually more than 7,000 words and less than 40,000 words.
On Acceptance:	writer is paid when editor accepts the finished work
On Publication:	writer is paid when the piece has been published.
POD:	print on demand (published as needed).
Query:	sometimes called a "pitch". Summary of a proposed work accompanied with sample chapters and synopsis.
Reprints:	previously published works.
Royalties:	a percentage of the cover-price of the book. This amount can sometimes be negotiated.
SASE:	Self Addressed Stamped Envelope sent to publisher to ensure return of manuscript.
Simultaneous:	manuscript sent to more than one publisher at a time.
Submission:	the action of presenting a proposal, application, or other document for consideration or judgement.
Synopsis:	a brief summary of the chapters and overall presentation of the work.
Tearsheet:	pages from newspaper or magazine that contained your work.
Unsolicited:	book, story, article, poem, etc. which was not specifically requested.
Work for Hire:	the work writer has been paid to do. Writer does not own the work or have any claims over it.

Membership Associations for Writers:

American Society of Journalists and Authors

Authors Guild

Association of Authors' Representatives

Garden Writers Association

Mystery Writers of America

National Association of Science Writers

National Education Writers Association

National Writers Union

Science Fiction Writers of America

Small Publishers, Artists and Writers Network

Writers Guild of America

Writer Conferences

FREE EXPRESSIONS SEMINARS AND LITERARY SERVICES
Workshops and Services for Dedicated Writers
Phone: (813) 391-8980
Fax: (813) 246-9020
www.free-expressions.com

THE WRITERS INSTITUTE
The University of Wisconsin
http://www.dcs.wisc.edu/lsa/writing/awi/index.html

GOTHAM WRITERS' WORKSHOP
Dana Miller, Director
555 Eight Avenue, #1402
New York, NY 10018-4358
Phone: 877-974-8377
Email: dana@write.org

ANTIOCH WRITERS WORKSHOP
Antioch Writers Workshop
P. O. Box 494
Yellow Springs, OH 45387
(937) 475-7357
http://www.antiochwritersworkshop.com/

SANTA BARBARA WRITERS CONFERENCE
Marcia Meier, Director
P.O. Box 6627
Santa Barbara, CA 93160
Phone: 805-964-0367 E-Mail: info@sbwritersconference.com
http://www.sbwritersconference.com

INDIANA UNIVERSITY WRITERS CONFERENCE
Bob Bledsoe, Director
Indiana University Writers Conference
464 Ballantine Hall
Bloomington, IN 47405
Phone: 812-855-1877
E-Mail: robledso@indiana.edu
Neil Perry, Associate Director: ndperry@indiana.edu
http://www.indiana.edu/~writecon/home.html

PIKES PEAK WRITERS CONFERENCE
Kirsten Akens, 2008 Director
Pikes Peak Writers Conference
4164 Austin Bluffs Parkway #246
Colorado Springs, CO 80918
United States
Phone: 719-531-5723
E-Mail: info@pikespeakwriters.com
http://www.pikespeakwriters.com

COLRAIN POETRY MANUSCRIPT
Joan Houlihan, Director
Writing Your Vision, "Making It Clear" 99
Concord Poetry Center
40 Stow Street
Concord, MA 01742
Phone: 978-897-0054
E-Mail: cpc@concordpoetry.org
http://colrainpoetry.com

Christian Writers Conferences:

Blue Ridge Mountains Christian Writers Conference

https://www.blueridgeconference.com/

Mount Hermon's Christian Writers Conference

Mount Hermon, California

http://www.mounthermon.org/

Write-to-Publish Christian Writers Conference

Wheaton College, Wheaton, Illinois

http://www.writetopublish.com/

North Texas Christian Writers Conference

Bedford, Texas

http://www.ntchristianwriters.com/

St. David's Christian Writers Conference

Geneva College, Beaver Falls, Pennsylvania

http://www.stdavidswriters.com/

American Christian Writers Conferences

Dates throughout the year, 27 cities across America.

www.acwriters.com

Places to Submit: Magazines/Journals/Newspapers

The Poetry Foundation

https://www.poetryfoundation.org/poetrymagazine/submit

First time poetry writing only; pays $10 per line

100 The Writers Guide

The Writers Weekly

http://writersweekly.com/writersweekly-com-writers-guidelines

Seek articles about home-based businesses and self-employment.

EzineArticles

http://ezinearticles.com/ - Emphasis on original articles on a variety of topics.

BusinessKnowHow

http://www.businessknowhow.com/

Focus on Small Business Strategies and best practices.

ArticleBiz

Interested in articles from any areas or topics.

ArticleAlley

http://articlealley.com/

Publish professional web articles on your favorite topics.

On-Line Resources

www.worldcat.org - a great resource that enables you to locate any books (including your own). Simply type the title to find out which library is carrying them.

www.copyright.gov/newsnet - provides general updates, licensing regulations and any new legislative developments.

www.writing.shawguides.com - provides a listing of writer conferences and workshops.

www.authorlink.com - this site is all about books, writing, and publishing.

www.Writing.Com - is the online community for writers and readers of all interests and skill levels.

http://www.apastyle.org/ - APA Style.org. APA publishes a number of books and guides designed to help you write in APA Style.

http://www.merriam-webster.com/ - Merriam-Webster dictionary on-line.

http://dictionary.reference.com/ - Dictionary/Thesaurus on-line.

http://www.writersdigest.com/writersresources - events and educational resources.

http://twitter.com - a great source for interacting and sharing ideas with published writers. Suggested tweets to follow include:

- @WritersDigest
- @AdvicetoWriters
- @LunaParkReview
- @NewYorker
- @LitRejections

WRITER'S FAQ'S

- **What's the best way to become a writer?** Though helpful, a degree in English, journalism or communication is not a necessary pre-requisite to becoming a writer. You will need the ability to put your ideas into words, a willingness to invest in time for reading and writing, and a have a determination to succeed. Attending writing workshops and conferences aren't mandatory, but advisable.

- **How can I find out information about various writing markets?** Search the web under keyword "writing markets". Several examples are listed below:
    ◊ **The Business Journal,** American City Business Journals, Inc, 96 North 3rd Street, Suite 100, San Jose, CA 95112 http://www.sanjose.bizjournals.com They pay on publication. They buy 300 nonfiction pieces a year that contain anywhere from 700-2,500 words, and they pay $175-$400 per piece. They suggest informing them of your interest to write for them either through phone or email.
    ◊ **Entrepreneur Magazine,** Entrepreneur Media, 2445 McCabe Way, Irvine, CA 92614. http://www.entrepreneur.com
    ◊ **My Business Magazine,** Hammock Publishing, 3322 West End Avenue, Suite 700, Nashville, TN 37203. http://www.mybusinessmag.com. My Business Magazine has a circulationOf 600,000 and was established in 1999. They are 75% freelancer written and accept queries by mail and fax. They will pay upon acceptance. They like non-fiction, how-to, and "new products" books. They accept literary pieces averaging 200-1,800 words, and they pay $75-$1,000 for each piece
    ◊ **The Network Journal,** Black Professional and Small Business News, The Network Journal
    ◊ Communication, 39 Broadway, Suite 2120, New York, NY 10006.
    ◊ **The Writer Magazine,** This magazine is dedicated to helping seasoned and aspiring writers by offering a straightforward presentation of information, instruction, and motivation. They are 90% freelanced. It is important to become familiar with a magazine before querying. Contact information: http://www.writermag.com/

How can I learn the skills needed to be a good writer? Attend writing workshops and conferences at least once or twice per year. Study various writing techniques. Volunteer to serve on newsletter committees and college newsprint staffs. Join and actively participate in writer groups.

How can I avoid rejection? You won't be able to avoid rejections. The key is not letting it affect your determination to keep writing and submitting.

- **When should I get an agent?** The best time to get an agent is once you have an offer from your publisher for submitted work. Another approach can be making direct contact with agents during writer conferences. You can "pitch" your book, understanding there's no guarantee they'll peak the agents' interest. Generally, unless already published, securing an agent is a challenge.

- **Can I be a full time freelance writer?** This is highly unlikely, at least initially. If you are just starting out, it's best to maintain another source of income while pursuing your writing career. In other words, "don't quit the day job" just yet.

Writers Podcast:

Moving From Vision to Print

www.anchor.fm/Theresa-Wilson

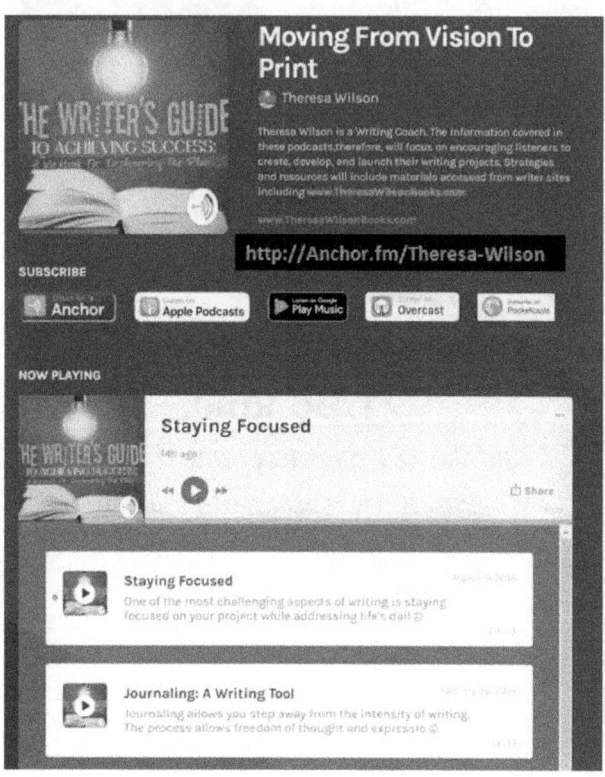

21/90 Rule:

It takes 21 days to create a habit.
It takes 90 dyas to create a lifestyle.

OUR ENDING...
YOUR BEGINNING...WRITE ON!

CONGRATULATIONS!
YOU ARE "IMPLEMENTING" YOUR PLAN!!

NEED ADDITIONAL SUPPORT?
Consider Our Writer's Coaching Program

- If you are looking for a personal breakthrough
- If you want to identify things that interfere with your success

How we deliver our Program:

PRE-ASSESSMENT
Coach Questionnaire call

PHASE 1 DELIVERY
-Assignments
-Goal Setting
-Journaling
-Feedback

PHASE 2 DELIVERY
-Teaching Techniques
-Individual Assignments

PHASE 3 DELIVERY
-Follow up based on results of Individual progress
-End of program one-on-one coachingand individual written assessment

For additional information about Writers in the Marketplace, visit:

Website: www.TheresaWilsonBooks.com
FaceBook: https://www.facebook.com/writersmarketplace/
Twitter: http://twitter.com/WritersCoach21
Podcast: http://anchor.fm/Theresa-Wilson

To order additional copies, or to arrange Workshops/Speaking Engagements and/or Coaching support, contact:

Speakers' Division
Writers in The Marketplace Press
P.O. Box 47182
Windsor Mill, MD. 21244
Email: theresawilsonbooks@gmail.com

Books Also Available On:

 &

About the Author

Theresa V. Wilson, M.Ed., is a writer and speaker who works to provide seminars and coaching-support to new and seasoned writers. She teaches participating writers to use 'learn-by-doing" techniques, which ultimately aids the writer in preparing their work for publication.

As a writing coach and group leader, Theresa provides one-on-one guidance for using effective strategies in addressing challenges that affect writing progression, while enabling individuals to focus on their unique strengths. Theresa's by-lines have appeared in over 80 online and print magazine publications. She was also a newsletter editor and faculty member for the American Christian Writers Association. Her media expertise includes moderating the "Small Minority Business Entrepreneurs" program of New Jersey Public Television.

Theresa was contributing author of the Guideposts book series and Penned from the Heart poetry, a production of Sunrise Press. Her other books include When Your Normal Is Upset: Living Secure in Uncertain Times, and Reaching, Searching, and Seeking: Letting the Spirit Lead book and audio CD. All of her books can be found on amazon.com and barnesandnoble.com.

www.ingramcontent.com/pod-product-compliance
Lightning Source LLC
LaVergne TN
LVHW061312060426
835507LV00019B/2118